Seeing and Believing
How to Teach Media Literacy in the English Classroom

ELLEN KRUEGER AND MARY T. CHRISTEL

Boynton/Cook
HEINEMANN
Portsmouth, NH

Boynton/Cook Publishers, Inc.
A subsidary of Reed Elsevier Inc.
361 Hanover Street
Portsmouth, NH 03801–3912
www.boyntoncook.com

Offices and agents throughout the world

The authors and publisher wish to thank those who have generously given permission to reprint borrowed material:

"Here's to the Crazy Ones" © Apple Computer, Inc. Used with permission. All rights reserved. Apple® and the Apple logo are registered trademarks of Apple Computer, Inc.

Library of Congress Cataloging-in-Publication Data
Krueger, Ellen, 1953–
Seeing and believing : how to teach media literacy in the English classroom / Ellen Krueger and Mary T. Christel.
        p. cm.
    Includes bibliographical references and index.
    ISBN 0-86709-573-3 (alk. paper)
    1. English language—Study and teaching (Secondary)—United States. 2. Motion pictures in education—United States. 3. High school students—Books and reading—United States. I. Christel, Mary T. II. Title.

LB1631 .K78 2001
428'.0071'273—dc21

00-050762

Editor: Lisa Luedeke
Production coordinator: Sonja S. Chapman
Cover design: Joni Doherty
Manufacturing: Deanna Richardson

Printed in the United States of America on acid-free paper
Docutech RRD 2006

To our families, our friends, our colleagues and administrators, our former and current students, our film studies mentors, Christine Heckel-Oliver, Ralph Amelio, Rich Fehlman, Millburn custodians Carlo, Michele, and John, our editor, Lisa Luedeke, the SHS computer lab staff, and most especially, Lori Myers, whose technical help was invaluable. To all, we thank you for your loving support and encouragement.

Contents

Foreword

What do Shakespeare's *King Lear*, Alfred Hitchcock, "The Wonder Years," and Apple Computer's "Think different" ad campaign have in common? All are springboards for exciting lessons in the classrooms of Ellen Krueger and Mary Christel. The courses, units, and lessons described in *Seeing and Believing: How to Teach Media Literacy in the English Classroom* are models of their type. Ellen and Mary honor the rich heritage of the traditional English curriculum and infuse it with the contemporary energy of media literacy in ways that powerfully engage their students.

Just as Americans have long had a love-hate relationship with the media, American educators have had an ambivalent attitude about the inclusion of media in the school curriculum. I think some opponents of media study sincerely believe that media texts are inherently inferior to classic literature. Still others think that it is wrong to take valuable class time to study material that students read or watch on their own. It has always seemed natural for me to include media study in the English classroom. For one thing, doing so provides ways for teachers to connect the world of the literary canon and formal composition with the media-rich world our students inhabit. Certainly our students avidly consume the media in their time outside of class. Their written compositions reflect the current slang and the "casual" grammar and syntax of advertising (often to our dismay, I'm sure). Their discussions of literature often draw parallels to the movies and television shows they watch or to the popular music they listen to. I suppose nowadays students talk of Web sites and 'zines as well, which is how it should be. They bring to us the world they live in; we bring to them texts they would never choose on their own, teach them to think critically and creatively about a wide variety of texts, to craft personal and analytical responses to the texts, and to develop the commitment and the habits of mind to continue their education throughout their lives.

Over the last thirty years, there has been a building movement to include media literacy in the school curriculum. One problem is that the phrase "media literacy" has meant various things to various groups—from "buyer beware" warnings that we are being manipulated into selling our souls to exhortations that "everything is a text." Over the last decade, a consensus has emerged among international English educators to use the definition of *media literacy* developed by the Intermediate and Senior Division of the Ontario Ministry of Education (*Media Literacy Resource Guide* 1989). According to the Ontario model, there are eight key concepts in students' development of media literacy: (1) All media are constructions. (2) The media construct reality. (3) Audiences negotiate meaning in media. (4) Media have commercial implications. (5) Media contain ideological and value messages. (6) Media have social and political implications. (7) Form and content are closely related in the media. (8) Each medium has a unique aesthetic form.

Within this tradition of a more rigorous and academic approach to including media in the English curriculum, Ellen Krueger and Mary Christel have created *Seeing and Believing*, which offers English teachers an extensive collection of units, lesson plans, writing assignments, and student projects—all tested and honed over the years in their classrooms.

Seeing and Believing moves logically from how to teach with single visual images, to how to teach the moving image, to how to integrate film and video in the English curriculum. There are chapters on teaching film as a support to teaching literature, teaching literary themes within film study, teaching a stand-alone film unit or course, and combining literature, composition, film, and television together. You can read from beginning to end for the logical progression of their concepts, or you can start where your immediate interests are—the units and lesson ideas are explained so well you won't be lost if you just jump in. I particularly appreciate the samples of student work and the students' written reflection on their work. Through them we learn not just that the lessons worked, but that they also made a difference in the students' lives.

I've never had the privilege of sitting in on one of Ellen's or Mary's classes with teenagers, but I have attended their numerous presentations at the conferences of the National Council of Teachers of English. Always they provide for their audience a solid rationale in national curriculum standard and in adolescent learning. Always they rush to include as many great teaching ideas as they can in the allotted time. Always I come away not only with a great set of lessons they have used but also inspired to apply their ideas to books and films I want to teach. And always I have a list of must-see movies and must-read books. So contagious is their enthusiasm for literature, film, and television, that I predict your reading of *Seeing and Believing* will be interrupted more than once by a trek to your neighborhood video store or public library.

Ellen and Mary are two of the most generous teachers you'll ever meet. With *Seeing and Believing* they roll their file cabinet into the back of your classroom, pull out folder after folder, and say things like: "The students really found this one interesting." "Look what they produced when we showed them *this* film!" "Shakespeare? Here's a thick file to help you there!" "Need a film to show with that unit on modern American short stories? Have you thought about this one? Or these television shows?" "Ideas about viewing guides? Still or moving? Okay, there's this way and this other way or you could . . ."

Seeing and Believing is better than going to a conference or attending a workshop. Thanks, Ellen and Mary! Our classrooms are the richer for your efforts.

—Alan B. Teasley, Ph.D.

Introduction

MARY T. CHRISTEL

*My task which I am trying to achieve is, by the power of the written word
to make you hear, to make you feel—it is before all, to make you see.*
—JOSEPH CONRAD

As novelist Joseph Conrad struggled to define the role of the fiction writer in the realm of high art in the late nineteenth century, the visual arts of photography and film were developing as popular culture, even as just novelties. The mission of early photographers and filmmakers echoed Conrad's, substituting "the written word" with "the image." Early silent filmmaker D. W. Griffith even appropriated Conrad's sentiments in his own manifestos, advancing the role of film to the realm of high art. Griffith's efforts to capture human experience on screen prompted President Woodrow Wilson to exclaim that he had seen "history written with lightning" as he watched *Birth of a Nation* (Williams 1980, 74). Early filmgoers were naive enough to accept what they saw on the screen as actual reality. They cowered in their seats when they saw a train bearing down on a camera placed in its path, believing they would risk bodily injury in the comfort of their theatre seats. Now we would claim that we are certainly more sophisticated viewers of visual media messages. We don't absolutely believe what we see. Or do we? Are we seduced by the beauty and pleasure of visual images—as well as the ease with which we can absorb them?

Our culture is without doubt a highly visual one. Most of the visual images we receive on a daily basis are transmitted through the media: television, film, advertising, magazines, newspapers, Web pages—the channels are proliferating. Because that flow of visual communication is so persistent and insistent, we have come to take them for granted, to dismiss their importance, to insist that they have no long-term impact on our perceptions of the world and ourselves. We certainly have not elevated those messages to a level of privilege, to make them even a partial focus in the language arts curriculum in United States schools, though schools in Canada, England, and Australia have worked to integrate media literacy initiatives as a matter of course in every student's experience. Media literacy here has been marginalized to special interest electives in journalism, TV production, film analysis, or photography. With the growing glut of media outlets and media messages, a need to equip a student, any and all students, to be able to analyze and respond to a media text critically becomes a vital component of language arts education, because the visual languages of media are even more difficult to negotiate than the written language of the traditional curriculum.

The National Council of Teachers of English (NCTE) has recognized the importance of studying media texts by drawing attention to their value in developing a well-rounded set of skills and providing a rich pool of resources for a language arts curriculum in the standards the council, in conjunction with the International Reading Association (IRA), published in 1996. Of the twelve standards, four directly address the need for developing critical competencies to analyze and create print and nonprint media:

> Standard No. 4: Students adjust their use of spoken, written, and visual language (e.g., conventions, style, vocabulary) to communicate effectively with a variety of audiences and for different purposes.
>
> Standard No. 6: Students apply knowledge of language structure, language conventions (e.g., spelling and punctuation), media techniques, figurative language, and genre to create, critique, and discuss print and nonprint texts.
>
> Standard No. 7: Students conduct research on issues and interests by generating ideas and questions, and by posing problems. They gather, evaluate, and synthesize data from a variety of sources (e.g., print and nonprint texts, artifacts, people) to communicate their discoveries in ways that suit their purpose.
>
> Standard No. 8: Students use a variety of technological and informational resources (e.g., libraries, databases, computer networks, video) to gather and synthesize information and to create and communicate knowledge. (Smagorinsky 1996, viii–ix)

Technology and the mass media present a gamut of new choices and challenges for the well-informed teacher and student. But the lack of attention to critically evaluating and creating texts produced through these technological advances diminishes the individual's ability to compete in future academic and workplace settings. The NCTE has issued a challenge through these standards: to prepare students to use technology effectively and critically to understand the texts produced by it. These standards require the integration of media texts with the same pedagogical rigor that is used to address literary texts.

Howard Gardner, by identifying the seven intelligences, in *Frames of Mind* (1983), defends the teaching of media as a way to tap into the levels of intelligence, such as spatial, musical, and bodily-kinesthetic, that a traditional language arts curriculum has often ignored. This study has given teachers theoretical permission to integrate nontraditional texts and analytical activities related to those texts in order to play to an individual student's academically nontraditional strengths and to expose other students to aspects of their intellect that need further development or exploration.

The improvement in and availability of video technology has also given teachers permission to use media texts creatively and responsibly. Sometimes our prejudices about using or not using media texts are based on our unsatisfying experiences in school. Remember the rented 16mm copy of *Pride and Prejudice* that arrived two weeks too early and that the class was forced to watch on a rickety projector with muffled sound before the syllabus even approached a discussion of Jane Austen? Or what about those scintillating film strips with sound that never quite synchronized with the image? For most schools, those days are gone forever. The advent of the VCR and videotape has opened up a whole range of possibilities and flexibility. The screening of a film now can be perfectly coordinated with a unit of study. It is easy to cue up a specific scene from a Shakespeare play, possibly from several different versions, to explore a difficult speech or to add greater clarity to a class discussion and student understanding.

The close analysis of the aesthetic, technical, or commercial qualities of media texts prepares students to produce their own media messages. The growing sophistication and affordability of home video equipment allows for expanded use of that technology in the schools and enables students to become makers, not just consumers, of high-quality media messages, a very important component of media literacy. Public access to cable programs and Web pages facilitate the dissemination of those messages to audiences broader than those in the immediate classroom setting. The trend toward giving students "real life" experiences in the language arts classroom comes to fruition in an extremely powerful way.

Once these cursory defenses of media literacy are in place, it is important to note that a teacher's desire to integrate media texts into the curriculum allows for a great deal of freedom and ingenuity, but therein lies most of the challenge and some measure of frustration. By and large, English/language arts teachers have little or no formal training in the analysis of media texts as compared with our training in literature and composition. Clearly, techniques can be transferred from the pedagogy of reading and writing to the analysis of print and nonprint media texts, but relying solely on those techniques doesn't fully reveal the potential and artistry of film, television, advertising, or journalism. Teachers need to become students of media industries to acquire the critical language to discuss, for example, film as a visual, rather than a narrative, text. Teachers need to critically evaluate the kinds of media texts that will be integrated into a unit and then carefully plan the critical strategies to analyze those texts with the same rigor they analyze any traditional written text. And finally, teachers will need to realize that some students may resist treating material that they deem as "entertaining," not "instructional." That resistance will melt away when students recognize how stimulating and relevant the discussion of media can be.

Ellen and I represent those teachers who were trained in a fairly traditional manner, but early in our teaching careers we found ourselves assigned to and interested in high school electives that required the close analysis of media texts. This book represents, collectively, forty-five years of experimentation in the classroom and involvement in media literacy training through all-too-limited conferences and coursework for high school teachers. Both Ellen and I have moved beyond the inclusion of media-focused activities only in specialized electives to the integration of those activities in traditional literature and composition courses. The activities compiled in this book have been used in our classrooms as well as shared with other teachers, who have further experimented with these techniques and have successfully integrated them into their own classes with the necessary modifications to make each activity their own.

As you move through the book, you will notice two distinct and complementary voices. I have tried to provide the framework for meaningful analysis in chapters that address terminology to examine still and moving images, offer strategies to help students master those concepts, and develop curricula that integrate media activities into standard literature classes and give students the opportunity to study film more intensively in an elective setting. Ellen writes from the immediacy of teaching units in media, literature, and writing classes during the school years when this book was being developed. She not only presents her rationale and lesson plans, but also integrates the responses of her students to help readers understand the impact of media analysis on critical thinking, literacy, and writing skills. We hope that, by providing readers with a broad range of concepts and their applications, we help them to encourage students not to see and passively believe, but to see in more active and meaningful ways, to question and analyze, and to make conscious decisions about what they believe.

Works Cited

GARDNER, HOWARD. 1983. *Frames of Mind: The Theory of Multiple Intelligences.* New York: Basic Books.

SMAGORINSKY, PETER. 1996. *Standards in Practice: Grades 9–12.* Urbana, IL: NCTE.

WILLIAMS, MARTIN. 1980. *Griffith: First Artist of the Movies.* New York: Oxford University Press.

ONE

Strategies of Visual Composition

MARY T. CHRISTEL

Most teachers do not feel comfortable examining visual images beyond their narrative quality simply because they do not have access to a practical set of terms that address aspects of visual composition in a systematic fashion. When I first started teaching a film course, I inherited a textbook called *Exploring the Film*. Long after the book has gone out of print and the copies in my classroom have fallen apart, I still use the five principles of visual composition from that textbook to begin any analysis of still and moving images. Beginning with still images helps both teacher and students look critically and thoughtfully at the image's composition, which prepares them for examining the images that stream past the viewer in a motion picture.

Defining Terms

In *Exploring the Film*, William Kuhns and Robert Stanley begin their discussion of visual composition with the concept of the *frame*. All images exist in a frame by virtue of being captured by a camera that has a limited field of vision. Within any framed image, there can be interior frames (1968, 49) that draw a viewer's eye to a particular aspect of the subject. These interior frames can consist of doors, windows, or geometric patterns that surround and highlight a person, object, or aspect of the environment.

Placement refers to the position of the camera in relationship to the subject. When examining placement the viewer must consider the distance between the camera and the subject. That distance can be described as a close-up, a medium shot, or a long shot (51). Depending on the distance between the camera and the subject, the viewer will be able to see that subject in the context of his environment or, as the camera increasingly isolates the subject from his surroundings, to concentrate on the subject's facial expression. Then the viewer must consider the angle of the camera, which can be high (placed above the subject) or low (placed below the subject). When examining the distance and angle of the camera, viewers need to consider how the position of the camera affects the viewer's impression of the subject. A high angle shot can make a subject look weak and dominated. A low angle, on the other hand, can make the subject look powerful and imposing.

Related to camera placement is *subject arrangement.* Arrangement is the relationship of the elements in the images that constitute the subject of the shot. The physical positioning of people and objects within a single shot can clearly establish the relationship, or lack of one, between them. Examining the arrangement of a shot also helps the viewer become aware of how he enters the image. Does the arrangement of a figure in the foreground of the image with her back turned to the viewer as she looks at a fire in the distance provide a similar pathway for the viewer to see what the subject sees? The viewer needs to consider what is placed in the foreground, middle ground, and background of a given image as well as how the elements in those planes work in harmonious and discordant ways. A single shot can also exploit the notion of the extended image. These are "incomplete images, images that are not whole unless the viewer mentally or emotionally fills them in, using the off screen space as a larger canvas" (Sobchack and Sobchack 1987, 79). Some images can have action spilling out of the frame or people looking at activity outside of the frame. Especially with the latter, the viewer can speculate about the nature of that activity based on the facial expressions and body language of the spectators.

Finally, the viewer needs to consider how *lighting* and *color* draw the eye to particular aspects of the image. The use of highly saturated or strong colors like red draw the eye to particular aspects of an image. In the composition of black-and-white images the values of gray in an image can be carefully orchestrated and potent indicators of importance. Lighting can train attention on aspects of a subject through the use of spot, concentrated, and diffused lighting. Both lighting and color can suggest a mood for a visual image. Examples drawn from print advertising offer some of the best examples of the manipulation of color and light to enhance the qualities of a product or the results of the use of that product.

To augment this basic approach to the analysis of a single static image, Louis Giannetti discusses the principles of the photographic image in the first chapter of his text, *Understanding Movies* (1998). He organizes his chapter around the following subtopics: Realism and Formalism; The Shots; The Angles; Light and Dark; Color; Lenses, Filters, etc. He ends the chapter with a discussion of the role of the cinematographer in the creative process and provides an impressive selection of color plates to illustrate his discussion of the various techniques. Depending on the sophistication and experience of the students, teachers certainly could modify the terminology used in this basic training.

Applying Concepts

Single-Image Analysis

In *Exploring the Film*, Kuhns and Stanley illustrate visual composition strategies with comic book strips. This is a good starting place, because the use of the composition

Shot		one image shot by one camera in one take, the basic unit of film
	sequence	a series of shots edited together to depict one event
	extended image	images that are incomplete within the frame of a single shot, which forces the viewer to "fill in" what exists outside the frame
1. Framing		limits the field of vision or draws the viewer's attention to a specific aspect of the shot
	interior	windows, doorways, arches, etc., that create framing devices within a shot
2. Arrangement		the physical relationship or position of people, objects, and background in a single shot
	foreground	field in the shot that is closest to the viewer
	middle ground	field that is between the foreground and background
	background	field that is farthest from the viewer
3. Placement		position of the camera in relationship to the subject of the shot
	distance	
	close-up	face, object fills the frame, greatly limiting viewer's field of vision
	medium shot	subject shown with some background context, usually figure shown from waist up
	long shot	subject shown with full background context
	angle	
	high	camera placed above the subject, usually makes subject look dwarfed, less powerful
	low	camera placed below the subject, usually makes subject look powerful
4. Lighting		
	spot	intense pool of light that isolates a small field of the shot, usually focused on a face, a key element of the subject of the shot
	concentrated	bright light source to draw attention to aspect of the shot
	diffused	lighting that is altered by fog, smoke, or a filter to create mood, to obscure an aspect of the shot
5. Color		
	saturation	intensification of a specific color within a shot

©2001 by Ellen Krueger and Mary T. Christel from *Seeing and Believing*. Portsmouth, NH: Heinemann.

Figure 1–1. *Strategies for Visual Composition*

strategies in this form are usually very pronounced, and most strips and comic books exploit the progressive movement from frame to frame that mimics the dynamic of frame-to-frame gradual movement of the motion picture.

Another way to begin discussing these concepts is with slides. Being able to discuss an enlarged image parallels the experience of examining an image projected by a film and allows for communal viewing and discussion. I have found the best images to discuss are those you can glean from photography books or exhibits of photography mounted by local museums (that way you don't need to shoot your own slides). Certainly you can use slides of paintings to discuss the five principles of visual composition, but depending on the level of photoreality of the images, you are not completely duplicating the experience of a filmic image.

QUESTIONS FOR VIEWING SLIDES

When I show slides, I always have students respond to questions about what they see prior to having the class discuss the image. We need to combat the passive orientation that some students have to examining visual images and begin to train students to make critical judgments about images that we tend to take for granted in our media-saturated culture. Here is a sample of questions that I pose:

- What is the first element of the image that you notice? What draws your attention to it?
- Close your eyes and look at it again. What do you notice on second viewing? Why is your eye drawn to that aspect of the image?
- Why are elements of the foreground, middle ground, or background the most dominant?
- How does lighting and/or color draw your attention to specific aspects of the image?

SUGGESTED ACTIVITIES

To reinforce the concepts after viewing and discussing series of slides, have students select print images that illustrate the five concepts. Have students select a series of five different images that highlight each of the five principles. Students then write an explanation on the back of the image, describing why a particular image best illustrates framing, placement, arrangement, lighting, and color. Students could also choose a sixth image that effectively incorporates all five principles, which could lead to a more extended analysis of their choice. When students come to class, they can share their choices in a small group and decide which of the images best illustrate the five principles.

Suggested by Ralph Amelio in a course I took through the American Film Institute, a more creative extension of this examination of the single shot would be to have students create a single photographic image that illustrates the control of the five principles. Students should submit the photograph with an analysis of the visual strategies that create emphasis or impact or have students exchange photographs to complete such an analysis.

Storyboards

In order to link the visual composition strategies to the narrative qualities of film, I have students storyboard a section of a short story, novel, or play. A storyboard is just a series of rectangular boxes that represent a single frame or image of a sequence of movements that create a scene. The simpler the sequence that they need to depict the better. Students should provide a brief description of the single image in a column next to their drawing using the terminology to explain the choices they made with the visual components and include details about lighting and color that are not so easy to render in the storyboard format.

In Giannetti's *Understanding Movies* (1998), he presents a storyboard rendition of the crop-dusting scene from Alfred Hitchcock's *North by Northwest* on pages 172 to 197. That sequence of images provides a convenient means to discuss how attention to framing, arrangement, and placement factors into developing a sequence of action from an actual production. Students will not be able to make judgments about color and lighting since the storyboard is rendered in simple black-and-white line drawings.

TWELVE-SHOT SEQUENCE ACTIVITY

A culminating activity for the development of storyboard images is to have students shoot a series of twelve still images that define a simple activity: pumping gas, frying an egg, applying eye makeup. Students plan their shots first in a sketched-out storyboard form, then move on to taking the photographs and mounting the series of shots in their proper sequence on a poster board. A written analysis of the process can also be integrated into the activity. I have assigned this activity in the following manner:

> You will be taking twelve photographs to depict a simple sequence of action: i.e., brushing your teeth, making a sandwich, fixing a flat tire. The twelve shots must depict the action in a visually logical and coherent fashion. You also must demonstrate attention to placement, arrangement, framing, and lighting. There must be at least three different angles or distances among the twelve shots.

> In order to avoid wasting film, you are going to create a simple storyboard on the attached forms [see Figure 1–2]. Elaborate artwork is not required—stick figures will do! You need to plan the distance and angle of the shot by penciling it in on the storyboard sheet. Since these are all-purpose storyboard sheets, ignore directions to indicate sound or editing.

> It is suggested that you use a Polaroid camera if you have access to one. This way there will be no surprises when the film comes back. If you are using standard film that requires developing, consider making several takes of the same shot in your sequence so you have a choice of images.

Sketch of shot

Provide a written description of shot (arrangement, placement, framing, lighting, color) below:

Figure 1–2. *Storyboard Form: Twelve-Shot Sequence*

Once you've gotten your pictures back, mount them in sequence on a poster or on a series of sheets of paper in their proper order.

As a final step, analyze your control of the camera and the images you've produced in a one-page, typed response. You can also examine the difficulties of this kind of assignment and how it will prepare you for making a live action video.

Now students can move on to examining these techniques in motion!

Screening a Sequence

SUGGESTED ACTIVITY

A final activity I suggest to reinforce this analysis of visual composition is to apply it to a scene from a film. The crop-dusting scene from *North by Northwest* is one of the best for this purpose. Instead of having students look for examples of all five techniques, assign groups of students a particular focus and then they can report their examples to the class at large. Having students look for too much too soon can be overwhelming and frustrating, especially in the transition from examining static to moving images. The crop-dusting scene can be paired with a similar scene from *The X-Files: The Movie* set in a cornfield at night to discuss the impact of a drastic change in lighting in creating suspense.

The film adaptation of Stephen King's novel *Dolores Claiborne* provides two powerful examples of the impact of camera placement on perspectives to limit or expand the viewer's understanding of what occurs in a particular sequence. The film opens with the camera placed at the bottom of a staircase. The camera reveals shadows cast on the wall showing two figures engaged in a struggle at the landing above, then a body tumbles down the stairs. After an abrupt cut to the kitchen, the camera is placed at an extreme, high angle above a woman, Dolores, who is frantically searching the kitchen. This choice in camera angle emphasizes her panic and creates a feeling of disorientation in the viewer. The scene cuts back to the staircase with Dolores poised with a marble rolling pin in hand above the body on the stairs. This sequence is repeated later in the film, but the second time the viewer sees the action from the top of the staircase, which clearly reveals the struggle between two women, and once again a body tumbles down the stairs (this time presented in shots from several angles on the staircase). The sequence doesn't cut as quickly from the event on the stairs to the kitchen, in order to reveal the conversation between Dolores and her employer, who lies on the stairs begging Dolores not to call the doctor. The employer implores Dolores to kill her. The second time the viewer sees Dolores in the kitchen the camera is placed at eye or waist level to give the action a more natural view compared to the high aerial shot of the first version. The sequence finishes in the same fashion as the first version with Dolores standing over the body on the stairs. It is clear that the placement of the camera in each of these sequences either obscures or clarifies the action and its context.

7

After acquiring and mastering these five basic elements of visual composition, students will have the ability to critically examine print images like newspaper and magazine advertising. Once students are truly comfortable analyzing on this level they can graduate to the more sophisticated elements of camera movement, editing, and sound in more complex film sequences, which will be discussed in Part II of this text.

Films Cited

Dolores Claiborne, 1995, Taylor Hackford, R, 131 min.

North by Northwest, 1959, Alfred Hitchcock, NR, 136 min.

The X-Files: The Movie, 1998, Rob Bowman, PG13, 120 min.

Works Cited

GIANNETTI, LOUIS. 1998. *Understanding Movies*. 8th ed. Englewood Cliffs, NJ: Prentice-Hall.

KUHNS, WILLIAM, AND ROBERT STANLEY. 1968. *Exploring the Film*. Fairfield, NJ: Cebco.

SOBCHACK, THOMAS, AND VIVIAN SOBCHACK. 1987. An *Introduction to Film*. Glenview, IL: Scott Foresman.

TWO

The Power of the Image: Think Different™

ELLEN KRUEGER

Borrowing from the 1998 Apple® computer ad slogan, "Think different," I want my students to think differently about images in the media and about how these images influence our experiences of people and events and our attitudes toward them. This chapter will provide a number of activities designed to promote critical viewing skills, an essential component of media literacy. These skills include: questioning what they see, analyzing content and representation, and evaluating the messages and values promoted in these images.

Using Political Cartoons

One simple yet engaging way to explore how meaning is conveyed through images is to examine *New Yorker* covers. Since one of the major principles of media literacy is that "all media construct reality," this activity will help students understand that something as simple as a magazine cover is really the artist's version of reality, and that we must explore the meaning of these powerful visual statements. The covers are easily accessible, brilliantly conceived, and generally provocative. One particularly provocative illustrator is Art Spiegelman, author of the 1992 Pulitzer Prize–winner, *Maus*. In a *New York Times* article, Joyce Wadler says Spiegelman is "seeking more than a smile from cartoons" (5 March 1999). The article focuses on his 8 March 1999 cover, which depicts a policeman in a 1930s-style cartoon, standing at a shooting gallery "41 shots 10 cents" firing at the images of a man on a cell phone, a small child eating an ice cream cone, and an elderly woman holding a cane. The cover clearly comments on the Amadou Diallo shooting in New York City. Diallo was a young, unarmed man who was shot over forty times and killed by New York City police. According to Spiegelman, the cover was "not meant to be an indictment of all policemen." However, as evidenced by the 250 police officers who picketed the *New Yorker* offices, they didn't see it that way. Spiegelman intentionally creates a disturbing picture of what has happened to the image of the police. He believes people should be offended by the police actions. He is "depicting an existing attitude," and creating his version of reality. When asked why comics attract us, Spiegelman replied, "They go directly to the id."

Because cartoons affect us on such a visceral level, students readily respond to the single images depicted on these covers, bringing their own life experiences to the act of deconstructing these images and engaging in high-level critical thinking. They question what they see and explore the timeliness and relevance of these powerful images, as in the Spiegelman illustration. In addition, they analyze the subject matter and the artist's style, exploring why, for example, a 1930s cartoon style was used. Finally, students evaluate the message conveyed. Has the image of the police changed from the friendly neighborhood cop to the sadistic bully? To what degree can a magazine cover affect attitudes? The possibilities for classroom discussions are endless. Every week there is a potential lesson. Other provocative *New Yorker* covers by Spiegelman include a Hasidic man kissing a black woman (15 February 1993), President Clinton being interviewed by the press (16 February 1998), and the Titanic sinking along with the Oscar statues (23 March 1998).

In addition to Art Spiegelman, *New Yorker* illustrator Blitt shows two young male sailors embracing in Times Square (17 June 1996). This image can be paired with the famous Alfred Eisenstaedt signature photograph showing a sailor kissing a nurse during the VJ-Day celebration in Times Square at the end of WWII. Students compare the public displays of intimacy in the '40s and '90s and the appropriateness of these images as cover art. They talk about gays in the military, the policy of "don't ask, don't tell." Moving from magazine covers, we open the discussion to how gays are portrayed in the media. Are they represented as human beings or are cultural stereotypes reinforced? Finally, they evaluate society's attitudes toward homosexuals today. Are we truly more tolerant or not? What values do we as a society possess and should we accept them or challenge them?

Edward Sorel, another frequent illustrator of *New Yorker* covers, features four images of women in his 9 May 1994 cover. One frame shows a mother and daughter making dinner together in 1934. The second shows a mother and daughter taking frozen food out of a freezer in 1954. The third shows the mother putting dinner into the microwave in 1974, and the fourth shows a working mother on a cell phone ordering Chinese take-out while the daughter watches TV in 1994. Has Sorel re-created the history of women in four simple images? Are they accurate? What do we learn about society and technology from these images? Are we better off in the '90s because we have cell phones and microwaves? At what cost to society do we advance technologically? Once again, students bring their own life experiences to the interpretation of these images, and lively discussions ensue.

The seemingly simple task of examining *New Yorker* covers becomes a higher-level lesson in critical thinking. No two people experience an image in quite the same way. Age, sex, ethnicity, and life experience contribute to the way we negotiate meaning with the media. Through active engagement, students can learn to think differently about the power of the image and reflect on their own interactions with visual messages.

Using Photographs and Videotapes

Photojournalism is another engaging way to encourage students to recognize how meaning is conveyed through the single image as well as to reinforce critical thinking skills. In today's world, photographic images are essential to news stories. They are dramatically connected to timely events, such as war, natural disasters, and celebrations, and often replace the printed word. These images can make us laugh and cry or think and remember. According to photography critic Andy Grundberg, "photojournalism is directed toward a large audience. Consequently, a photojournalist's picture must always be accessible, eye-catching, and even provocative. They compete with words and other images for our attention, so they need to engage us almost viscerally. They commonly accomplish this in two ways: by appealing to the eye and by telling a story. They work visually and emotionally." Young viewers, in particular, rely on visual information much more than the printed word. With all the competition in the news industry (network, cable, Internet), editors must rely on visual devices to attract viewers. Cameras appear on the scene almost immediately to provide up-to-the-minute reports to the public. As Henry Luce, publisher of *Life* magazine, once said, "To see life; to see the world." His magazine popularized the photo essay and emphasized pictures that told stories. As teachers of media, we must help our students carefully interpret the images they see. Although photographs and videotapes appear to show reality, they are really just a version of reality, which are carefully processed before they appear in print or on the air. Students are rarely aware of this. It is important to explain that the images we see are filtered through the eyes of the producers and editors of the news before we even buy a newspaper or turn on our TV sets. Another principle of media literacy is that the media construct reality using a variety of techniques that cleverly manipulate audience response. By examining these techniques, we are less susceptible to their power. Topics to think about relating to TV news broadcasts are

1. the selection order of stories chosen for that day;
2. the amount of time devoted to covering each story;
3. the role of the anchor person in the studio;
4. the use of location shots and file footage;
5. the editing of the images to fill the available time slot;
6. the music;
7. the use of graphics such as charts, statistics, and station logos;
8. the camerawork; and
9. the choice of commercials used to sponsor the broadcast.

All these components work together to package the news. The presentation clearly affects our perception of the events and issues. Similar considerations exist in deconstructing the single image in print. Obviously, the way the image is shot and framed is a direct reflection of the point of view of the photographer. After all, there is no such thing as an objective photograph. The study of photojournalism encourages a study of current as well as historical events.

Looking back on controversial news stories that most students remember is a good place to begin. In a 10 May 1992 article in the *New York Times*, Charles Hagen critiques the videotaping of Rodney King being beaten and kicked by police officers "as defining evidence of the state of American society today." As described by Hagen, this videotape was shot at night from a distance. "The blurry, shaky tape reduces the event to a primal scene with the terrible power of nightmare, as the shadowy figures of the police lash out at the prone figure of Mr. King, caught in the white glare of headlights." This footage, played repeatedly on television, assaulted the senses of the American viewing public. No single photograph could so successfully have conveyed the impact of this event, yet the issue of interpretation is just as significant, as evidenced by the verdict in this case. Most people judged the tapes as evidence of police brutality; however, the jury who acquitted the police saw it differently. Hagen's opinion is that photographic images must be "anchored in a convincing narrative before they take on specific meaning." Different readings of events illustrate the enormous power of the video image to sway public opinion.

A good way to begin a discussion of photojournalism is to ask students what they think the role of the photojournalist should be in society. Are they merely "reporters with a camera," or are they helping to shape the news? Should they try to heighten public awareness and promote social change, or simply record the events they were sent to cover? During the Depression, photographers hired by the Farm Security Administration were sent out to document the lives of ordinary Americans such as coal miners and migrant workers. These powerful images by such notables as Walker Evans and Dorothea Lange were especially effective in promoting social change. Photographs taken during the early years of WWII, of women working in nontraditional fields were used to promote nationalism. With today's technology, however, photography has moved beyond documentation. Lighter cameras, faster film speeds, and more powerful lenses help photographers create more personal, intimate images.

ACTIVITY FOR "READING" PHOTOGRAPHS

One activity that will help students "read" images more closely is to ask them to select a photograph that they feel is visually effective from a current news or feature story in a newspaper or news magazine. Students cut out the photo and mount it on a piece of paper. The caption is cut off and taped to the back of the sheet. Carefully examining the images, students think about what visual information it contains. In a fully developed written paragraph, students explain why they chose their particular photograph. Was it because of the camerawork? In terms of placement, were the images shot from an interesting angle or extremely close up? How were the images arranged within the frame? What may have been eliminated? What effect did they create? How about the lighting? Does it dramatically enhance the images? Does the photograph have emotional appeal? The next day in class, students form small groups. Each mem-

Important website 10/31/07
www.hagginmuseum.org

ber shows his or her photo to the other members of the group and remains silent while they are examining it. The group is asked to respond to the "visual cues" out loud, pointing to specific examples of camerawork (shots and angles), framing, lighting, and the overall emotional appeal of the photograph. Then they decide how the camerawork has affected their experience of the image. Are they moved, saddened, angered, or amused by what they see? At this point, the presenter may join the discussion and share similar or different reactions. Finally, the group should try to determine what story the photo accompanied. The presenter then reads the caption describing the event. The caption will shed light on how the event has been interpreted by the news source. For example, one of my students brought in a photo of two Palestinian youths firing slingshots at Israelis while a Palestinian stands behind them, smiling. After the group analysis has been concluded, the entire class comes together to address the issue of how photographic images influence our perceptions of issues and how we can become more sensitized to the process by which the news is filtered.

Using Pulitzer Prize–Winning Photographs

Another effective way to examine how images influence our perceptions of issues is by looking at Pulitzer Prize–winning photographs. Three excellent sources are *Moments: The Pulitzer Prize Photographs*, by Shery and John Leekley; *Moments* by Hal Buell; and a 1999 TNT documentary titled *Moment of Impact: Stories of the Pulitzer Prize Photographs*. These emotionally potent, provocative photographs document the history of our country for posterity. Several award winners that have created these lasting impressions come to mind: the flag being raised at Iwo Jima, the shooting of Lee Harvey Oswald, the girl crying over the dead body at Kent State University, and the children crying from napalm burns running down the road in Vietnam. As the photographer pressed the shutter of his camera, a moment of history was immortalized. I begin the unit by asking my students what qualities they feel should be captured in a photograph that wins a Pulitzer Prize. Some sample student responses include: "They should reveal layers of meaning and make you look, feel, and think," and "they should remind you of events if you were alive, or bring you to events if you weren't alive."

QUESTIONS FOR VIEWING PRIZE-WINNING PHOTOGRAPHS
A viewing activity that will help students think critically is to show these images and have students look for the same "visual cues" as they did in the photojournalism assignment. As each image is presented on a transparency, students should jot down their impressions, giving careful attention to the following criteria:

1. What do you notice about placement, the way the photograph was shot and from what angle?
2. What exactly do you see within the frame?

3. How was the photograph arranged?
4. What might have been cropped in the editing process?
5. How does the lighting enhance the image?
6. How does the use of black-and-white or color film convey a desired effect?

Another area to analyze is the subjective experience of the viewer. Students should be encouraged to describe how they feel about what they see. How does the image affect their experience of the event? Finally, on an evaluative level, discuss what messages/values are inherent in a single image? Does the photo of the soldiers raising the flag on Mount Suribachi symbolize patriotism, freedom, pride, or triumph? Does the image of the burned children running make a powerful antiwar statement? Did the photo of the slain student at Kent State University denounce the "establishment"? Students will bring their own life experiences to these discussions and shed light on their own sets of values and beliefs. After an extensive study of these frozen moments of time, one of my students summarized her feelings by saying, "The Pulitzer Prize–winning photographs are like classics in literature . . . they are well-known, recognizable, and acclaimed. When you tell a news story with no words, your imagination is free to roam." Clearly, this student has experienced the power of the image. Another principle of media literacy is that the media contain ideologies, values, and messages. Photographers present their versions of reality, and their points of view, every time they look through the lens. Students need to address the subtle or overt messages captured in these images and decide for themselves whether or not they share these beliefs.

Exploring the Power of Images Through the "Think Different" Campaign

A third way to heighten student awareness and to explore the power of the single image is by deconstructing a recent ad campaign mounted by Apple Computer, Inc. In 1998, Apple Computer created an ad campaign that features national and international icons, both historic and contemporary, including Albert Einstein, Amelia Earhart, the Dalai Lama, and Lucille Ball. These people represent fields as diverse as science, aviation, human rights, and entertainment. Analyzing this campaign can launch discussions about the advertising industry, cultural literacy, the value of thinking differently, and the recognition of achievement.

When I asked Sarah, a student in my Mass Media class, to reflect on the Apple "Think different" campaign, she wrote, "I think the campaign is brilliant . . . it may not sell me a computer, but it has made me think about breaking barriers, breaking stereotypes, being different, and not conforming . . . the slogan is a simple one, but it brings up complex ideas." This lesson fosters critical thinking skills and shows the influence of one advertising campaign. It will actively involve students in lively classrooms discussions.

CLASSROOM ACTIVITIES FOR THE "THINK DIFFERENT" CAMPAIGN

This exercise can be used in English, art, science, music, and humanities classes to encourage students to investigate an array of people who have helped advance the human race. Since the purpose of the activity is to encourage students to recognize the power of the image, a good place to begin is with the images themselves. The images can be found in the *New Yorker, Premiere, Entertainment Weekly, Harpers,* and *Time.* Making transparencies is a practical idea. The order of presentation can be random or planned; however, each image should appear on the screen long enough for the students to complete the assigned task. Use the following guidelines for each image:

1. Examine the visual language of the ad.
2. Can the students identify each face?
3. What do students notice about the layout of the shot, including: framing, placement, arrangement, lighting, and use of black-and-white film?
4. Analyze the image.
5. Why do students think each of these faces was chosen?
6. What do these people have in common?
7. Evaluate the values/messages.
8. Beyond the product, the computer, what is actually being sold in this ad (creativity, rebellion, innovation)?
9. Will these associations "sell"?

Because many of the faces may be unfamiliar to high school students, a good suggestion for homework is to encourage students to use the Internet to supplement their own knowledge of these individuals. Students should bring their findings to class the next day. For example, on <http://www.celebsite.com>, one of my students discovered that Lucy and Desi owned their own production company, Desilu.

Review each image and have students share their thoughts. This is the most engaging part of the activity because students are anxious to share their readings of the visual text. For example, student responses to Lucille Ball and Desi Arnaz varied. Although almost everyone identified them as a popular 1950s TV couple starring in the long-running *I Love Lucy* show, some students made more astute observations. For instance, one student commented that Lucy and Ricky were an interracial couple who challenged the wholesome image of the 1950s. We reflected on how TV portrayed family life in 1950s sitcoms, and the images were entirely white and middle class. Another mentioned that Lucy was an outspoken housewife who wanted more than the confines of her apartment afforded her. She didn't want to be repressed by her husband. I added that Lucy's behavior appealed to numbers of frustrated housewives of the era who lived vicariously through her comical antics. She defied the limits of gender and dared to be different.

Additional reading can be done in David Halberstam's *The Fifties* (1993), which reports that executives at CBS studios were less than enthusiastic about casting Desi

Arnaz as Lucy's TV husband. His was not a household name and because of his Cuban accent, his English was not strong. The executives claimed no one would accept the premise that Lucy was married to a Cuban bandleader. "What do you mean nobody will believe it . . . we are married," Lucy emphatically stated (197). The show went on to earn strong ratings for CBS and a profit for the network. From my own research, I discovered that it is generally believed that more people watched the episode of the birth of little Ricky on January 19, 1953, than the inauguration of Dwight Eisenhower the next day. The consensus of the class was unanimous. Lucy and Ricky were ideal choices for this campaign. By choosing them, Apple is selling the notion of challenging the established system. They were people who went against the grain.

Another face in the campaign was Pablo Picasso. Students had a far more difficult time recognizing him. I laughed as they guessed he was everyone from Henry Kissinger to the Pope to John Glenn. Once they realized who he was, they carefully examined the extreme close-up shot of his face and concluded it was quite effectively photographed. He looked intense and contemplative. Most of the students identified Picasso as the artist who was responsible for the cubist movement in twentieth-century art. "He did weird stuff . . . he mixed things up a bit." Some students had even studied Picasso in their humanities class and could discuss the innovations of cubism. "He deviated from the norm and changed the way people thought about the human form and conventional perspective." One student enthusiastically referred to the "strippers" from *Les Demoiselles d'Avignon*. Another claimed that Picasso captured things as he saw them. The class thought Picasso was a good choice for the campaign because he saw things differently, and the Apple company is selling a "mind-set" as well as computers. The students realized Apple is doing something different with computer technology, and the message is, so can consumers if they buy this product.

After analyzing the choices of the Dalai Lama, John and Yoko, and Gandhi, the students realized some commonalities exist among the disparate group. Achieving self-rule for their people was important to both the Dalai Lama and Gandhi. Both men devoted their lives to winning independence for their countries, and both were advocates of nonviolent protest. Some students remembered studying Thoreau in tenth-grade American literature, and were able to reflect on his teachings and how they influenced twentieth-century peace movements. At this point, the Apple Computer campaign itself was hardly a part of the active discussion in the classroom. The film *Gandhi*, starring Ben Kingsley, was mentioned, and I brought up Uma Thurman's father, who is a scholar as well as a professor of Tibetan studies in New York. With regard to John Lennon and Yoko Ono, most of the students were more familiar with Lennon's murder than with what he represented in the '60s peace movement. With the help of the Internet, once again, one student discovered that the lyrics "give peace a chance" became the national anthem for the pacifists. In addition, the Internet provided information on how Lennon and Ono, instead of organizing boycotts or marches, staged "bed-ins" and invited the press to film and interview them while they shared their views on love and peace. One student associated Lucy and Desi with John and Yoko because both couples were involved in interracial marriages and saw the world differently. Eventually, the discussion addressed the question of what is being sold in this ad. Chris offered a comment that made the class pause and reflect. He said that through music, John and Yoko shared their worldview, just as the Apple Computer company, through its campaign, shares its worldview of creative people who have made changes.

Two additional faces in the collection are Jackie Robinson and Caesar Chavez. Unlike the extreme close-up shots of most of the celebrated faces, Robinson is shown from a high angle shot as he crosses home plate and simultaneously is shown shaking a white team member's hand. According to Ben, just as Robinson "crossed the plate" he "crossed the color barrier" and changed the course of professional baseball forever. Robinson was one of the most accessible faces to the students, unlike Caesar Chavez, whom none of them recognized. The Internet provided some biographical information on Chavez's involvement organizing the Farm Workers Union in 1966 to help secure the rights of migrant workers. Just as his predecessors the Dalai Lama, Gandhi, and Martin Luther King, Jr. (who is also represented in the Apple campaign), Chavez was a champion of nonviolent protest, who organized a grape boycott in 1968 that resulted in improved labor contracts for the workers. Seeing similarities among people of all races, socioeconomic backgrounds, political agendas, and creative contributions is truly a testimony to the great value of this campaign. The students unanimously agreed.

At the end of the discussion of all the celebrated faces, I asked my students to respond to the following prompt: What are you left thinking about after analyzing the Apple "Think different" campaign? Kristen offered, "Each person basically did something out of the ordinary, and I think that's what they are trying to say about the computer . . . it's different, not like anything else . . . it's bold and innovative." Jessica focused her response on the power of the campaign by commenting, "I find it interesting that you can take a famous person who is well-known for something, place him or her in an ad for a product, and how amazing it is that consciously or unconsciously the public connects the themes to the product being sold." Annie was much more critical of the effectiveness of the campaign: "I think the campaign uses great images and makes me want to think differently, but as far as buying an Apple computer, I don't think it's that convincing. I'm left thinking more about people's accomplishments in the twentieth century." Jon's response was more severe. "I think it's a brilliant campaign. Unfortunately, it leaves me with no knowledge of the product. As an informed consumer, I use ads for exposure to new products. I don't need a clever ad to convince me, just tell me about the product . . . this campaign appeals to the computer illiterate, who can be influenced without knowing the product." The most dissident reaction was from Ted, who described the campaign as "insidious." He believes that by "using famous figures from contemporary history, Apple had deified their 'different' computers, and made owning one a status symbol in one move . . . The new Macs® are nothing more than a status symbol for baby boomers who need someone to tell them they're still hip." Student responses range from respectful to contemptuous, yet the very nature of the disparate views makes this an exciting lesson.

STUDENT ASSESSMENT: CHOOSING THE NEXT FACE PROJECT
The final assessment I do is to ask students to select the next face for the campaign. They must carefully consider who should be celebrated for creativity in keeping with the vision of the campaign. Each student is responsible for creating an 8½-by-11-inch black-and-white display including the Apple logo and "Think different" slogan, which can easily be downloaded from the Apple Website. In addition, the students must write formal persuasive essays defending their choices. Student responses have included: John Coltrane, James Dean, Madonna, Bill Gates, Bob Marley, Beck, Nelson Mandela, Golda Meir, Walt Disney, Alfred Hitchcock, Philip Glass, Mark Twain, George Lucas, Sigmund Freud, Salvador Dali, Charlie Chaplin, and Stanley Kubrick. Ben explained his choice of Hitchcock: "He was an innovative, free thinker who bucked the system. He was a revolutionary force . . . a pioneer in various cinematic techniques who inspired a new generation of filmmakers. He was eccentric, demanding, inventive, and impassioned. Apple, too, is an innovative, free-thinking company, not afraid to go against the norms of the computer industry . . . additionally, by buying an Apple computer, you, too, can be an iconoclast." Clearly, Ben understands what the campaign is really selling. In a similar vein, Ted says Philip Glass "is the perfect model of a revolutionary . . . he is misunderstood . . . he shares many of the traits of the other 'Think different' spokespersons: originality, free thought, and a true sense of individuality. Maybe, after his death, people will look at him the way we look at his predecessors and realize that he was a genius ahead of his time." There is no question, regardless of whether students believe that the campaign celebrates or denigrates these individuals, that the "Think Different" lesson generates lively, provocative discussions.

A final activity is to show the sixty-second commercial that aired on prime time, which can be downloaded from the Apple Website. The text actually sounds like poetry and could certainly be treated as such in the classroom:

Here's to the Crazy Ones

Here's to the crazy ones.

The misfits.

The rebels.

The troublemakers.

The round pegs in the square holes.

The ones who see things differently.

They're not fond of rules.

18

And they have no respect for the status quo.

You can praise them, disagree with them, quote them,

disbelieve them, glorify or vilify them.

About the only thing you can't do is ignore them.

Because they change things.

They invent. They imagine. They heal.

They explore. They create. They inspire.

They push the human race forward.

Needless to say, my students have negotiated their own meanings with this campaign. They have questioned its premise, analyzed the aesthetic presentation of the images as well as the connections between the images and the product, and evaluated the messages and values being sold. As Ben said of Alfred Hitchcock, "he was not afraid to think different," and neither are my students.

Examining images in the media is an effective way of promoting critical thinking skills. Students discover how the media construct reality and learn that it is our responsibility as consumers of the media to develop the skills by which we can effectively read and evaluate these images and their messages. Each of us brings so much of our life experience to reading images that it helps us to use them to provoke discussions and encourage analysis of our media environment.

Additional Activities

The following activities explore images in different applications.

1. In order to foster an understanding of photographic techniques, have students find examples of engaging photographs from newspapers and magazines. They must identify the techniques (see Chapter 1), such as shots taken from low or high angles, and explain how these create a desired effect. Encourage them to express their views in writing. It is always helpful to model the assignment first.

2. Making stories from pictures is an exercise in perception. Using photographs from a variety of sources (newspapers, magazines, comics, Internet), students create a story with no words. This assignment requires several days because students may have to search for just the right image. Place the pictures sequentially so that anyone looking at it will be able to "read" the story. In class, the students form small groups and read each other's stories aloud. Different "readings" of the same text will ensue. This is the idea behind the project. People perceive images and the juxtaposition of images in different ways. Encourage students to share their creative processes with each other.

3. Define icon. Ask students to find icons that they believe have meaning. Consult magazines, newspapers, and computer images. The icon should be mounted on a sheet of paper and accompanied by a written defense. Students should be prepared to share their responses with the class. Popular icons are the bald eagle, the Nike swoosh, an illustration of a Norman Rockwell Thanksgiving, the Statue of Liberty, Coke bottles, Snoopy, the Olympic rings, and the Marlboro man.

4. Advertising is pervaded with images showing the "good life." Find an ad that creates this illusion. Discuss the images that contribute to this sales pitch. Then discuss what the ad neglects to tell us about the good life.

5. From discussions of literature, students usually study the powerful effect of language on the reader, from the lyrical prose of F. Scott Fitzgerald to the mundane realism of Arthur Miller to the concise, witty satire of Dorothy Parker. Encourage students to recognize that filmmakers such as Oliver Stone and Mike Nichols tell stories and create desired effects through images. They make conscious choices regarding camerawork, lighting, sound, color, and editing. An alternative assessment (instead of a conventional test) to a literature unit might be to select a theme—such as alienation, appearance versus reality, lost youth, or the American dream—and to ask students to tell a story illustrating that theme without using words.

Works Cited

BUELL, HAL. 1999. *Moments*. New York: Black Dog & Leventhal Publishers.

GRUNDBERG, ANDY. "Photojournalism: Heroism Meets Esthetics." *New York Times* 26 November 1989: II, 35:1.

HAGEN, CHARLES. "The Power of the Video Image Depends on the Caption." *New York Times* 10 May 1992: 32.

HALBERSTAM, DAVID. 1993. *The Fifties*. New York: Villard Books.

LEEKLEY, SHERYLE, AND JOHN LEEKLEY. 1978. *Moments: The Pulitzer Prize Photographs*. New York: Crown Publishers, Inc.

WADLER, JOYCE. "Seeking More Than a Smile from Cartoons." *New York Times* 5 March 1999: B2.

THREE

Cultural Diversity: Representation of Gender and Race in the Media

ELLEN KRUEGER

On November 1, 1999, at 9:00 P.M., Ford Motor Company bought an estimated ten million dollars of air time to run a two-minute commercial on dozens of national, regional, and cable channels throughout America as well as on overseas networks. In addition, the commercial appeared on two Websites. Known within the advertising industry as "roadblocking" (showing the commercial to millions of viewers at the same time), Ford boldly reached out to the public to celebrate diversity and to sell the Ford image. The two-minute spot featured footage that was filmed in nine countries and showed people representing different races and nationalities engaged in the business of ordinary life. Interspersed throughout the scenes were images of seven different Ford cars. Two important media issues arise from this campaign. The first is the attempt of advertisers to reach millions of viewers in an era with so many hundreds of competing channels to watch, and the second is the selling of a company's image by promoting racial, gender, national, and marginal group representation. Ford is a global corporation and, through this commercial, fosters worldwide appeal by selling trust and concern for its customers' lives. Regardless of whether the commercial was a stunt or an innovation, it provided valuable teaching moments in my unit on representation in the media. The unit described in this chapter will provide strategies to help prepare students to analyze, evaluate, and produce media messages.

The unit objectives are: (a) to analyze how gender and race are represented in the media; (b) to examine the relationship between media and society; (c) to explore how images in the media convey powerful meaning and affect our views of others and ourselves; (d) to question what else is being "sold" besides the product; and (e) to create visual images that reflect personal values. See Figure 3–1 for descriptions of techniques frequently used by advertisers.

1. *GLITTERING GENERALITIES*
   Speaking in broad, sweeping terms without specific qualifications: "Clinical studies prove that four out of five people lost weight successfully with Dexatrim."

2. *TRANSFER*
   Transferring ideas and emotions from one thing to another: "Tommy Hilfiger designs clothes for men that are as classic as a '55 Thunderbird."

3. *TESTIMONIAL*
   Endorsement by a well-known individual or organization: Michael Jordan featured holding a bottle of Gatorade.

4. *WORD MAGIC*
   Choosing words with high positive or negative emotional appeal: Calvin Klein's Obsession or Eternity.

5. *BARGAIN PRICES*
   Suggesting that someone's price is lower than one's competitors: "With these low-priced videos, you don't have to make a compromise." (Wal-Mart)

6. *PLAIN FOLK*
   Using ordinary people to endorse products: "For every expression there's a Toyota."

7. *SNOB APPEAL*
   Appealing to the desire for status: "Seize the day." (Jaguar)

8. *BANDWAGON*
   Suggesting that everyone else is doing it, and you should too: "The shoes America grew up in." (Keds)

9. *FACTS AND FIGURES*
   Implying that statistical facts and figures prove a point: "Soluble fiber from oatmeal as part of a low saturated fat, low cholesterol diet, may reduce the risk of heart disease." (Quaker Oats)

10. *CARD STACKING*
    Overemphasizing favorable points while deemphasizing the unfavorable: All cigarette and alcohol ads.

11. *HIDDEN FEARS*
    Playing upon the individual's insecurities: "No power. No radio. No land in site. Don't you wish you bought a Diehard."

12. *DIRECT ORDER*
    Appealing to the desire in people to be told what to do (imperative statements): "Just do it." (Nike)

13. *REPETITION*
    Repeating an idea in order to instill it in a person's mind: "New lemon Fantastik . . . combined with a refreshing lemon scent . . . nothing else cleans with the fresh scent of lemon."

©2001 by Ellen Krueger and Mary T. Christel from *Seeing and Believing*. Portsmouth, NH: Heinemann.

Figure 3–1. *The Language of Commercial Advertising*

Cultural Literacy for Students

According to Professor James Twitchell of the University of Florida, "advertising has become our cultural literacy—it's what we know" (1996). I was quite disturbed by this statement, yet resigned to accept its truthfulness. Wanting to introduce my unit on representation in an unconventional way, I designed a cultural literacy quiz (see Figure 3–2). My goal was to prove to students that print and television advertising have a powerful impact on our lives. I consulted *The Dictionary of Cultural Literacy* for two dozen questions representing literature, philosophy, history, and language. The quiz involved matching terms and phrases such as "Big Brother is watching you," with the proper identifier, George Orwell. Out of a group of forty, only a handful of students earned a perfect score, and many erred on three to eight questions (see answer keys on p. 38). Then I devised a second quiz, reflecting TV commercials, with questions such as, "name three types of music used in recent Gap commercials." Every student correctly produced swing, rock-and-roll, and country. Most students earned a perfect score on the second quiz (see Figure 3–3). Some were embarrassed that they were so proficient in recalling advertising slogans and jingles. The discussion that followed the quizzes proved to the students that, indeed, they were more literate when it came to pop culture because of their exposure to countless hours of print and TV advertising —approximately 1,500 ads pers day, according to media experts. With this realization in mind, students were sensitized to the power of the media to affect their lives without them being aware of it.

The Ad and the Ego

Another preliminary activity was to show the documentary *The Ad and the Ego*, which explores the cultural impact of advertising on individuals and on the way they see the world. To encourage active viewing, students were instructed to jot down observations, reactions, or questions they had to launch our discussion. Using 1,200 commercials in a fifty-seven-minute documentary, the film assaults the senses with a barrage of images of men and women hawking consumer products. Showing any portion of the documentary is adequate because the salient points are clearly presented throughout the film. For example, students' comments reflected a critical understanding of gender issues. Chrissy wrote, "each and every day, men and women are told by advertisers that they are not tall enough, thin enough, smart enough, or rich enough. If we would only use their shampoo, wear their clothes, or drive their cars, we would be perfect. Advertising focuses on people's insecurities and makes us feel uncomfortable about ourselves. They tell us that salvation is found in the consumer goods they sell." Focusing specifically on individual gender issues, Chrissy noticed that women on TV are young, happy, healthy, beautiful, and sexy, but at the same time, airbrushed and covered with makeup. Their flawlessness presented a skewed image of the average woman. Men, she noticed, were also prey to the advertising industry. "When the average stressed-out, balding family man is exposed to men on TV, he is forced to face his own glaring inadequacies in light of these flawless Ken dolls." Another

Cultural Literacy Quiz 1

Match the definition in column B to the term it defines in column A.

	A		B
___	1) Book of Genesis		a) guarantees women's right to vote
___	2) Adonis		b) a Chinese philosopher
___	3) Camelot		c) a pledge taken by doctors
___	4) Grim Reaper		d) a warning from Orwell's *1984*
___	5) R.S.V.P.		e) the beginning and the end
___	6) carpe diem		f) the Church of Jesus Christ of Latter-day Saints
___	7) Mona Lisa		g) a figure commonly used to represent death
___	8) American Gothic		h) an obsessive and unscrupulous pursuer of women
___	9) Vatican		i) Theodore Geisel
___	10) Allah		j) an acronym for White Anglo Saxon Protestant
___	11) in loco parentis		k) an incident during Nixon's presidency
___	12) 19th amendment		l) in the beginning God created the heavens and the earth
___	13) Archie Bunker		m) painting of a woman with a mysterious smile
___	14) Hippocratic Oath		n) an independent state within the borders of Rome
___	15) WASP		o) repondez s'il vous plait
___	16) Mormons		p) an American author known for his stories of poor boys becoming rich
___	17) Don Juan		q) seize the day
___	18) Confucius		r) King Arthur's kingdom
___	19) yin and yang		s) name for God in Islam
___	20) Horatio Alger		t) an American painting by Grant Wood
___	21) Big Brother is watching you		u) the father in *All in the Family*
___	22) Dr. Seuss		v) to assume duties and responsibilities of parents
___	23) Watergate		w) two forces in the universe
___	24) alpha and omega		x) any handsome young man

Figure 3–2.

Cultural Literacy Quiz 2

1. Name a type of dance/music used in a Gap khakis commercial.

   _____

2. Name a celebrity used in a "Got Milk?" ad.

   _____

3. What vodka celebrates its own image in clever ads?

   _____

4. Cite the Nike slogan. Draw the Nike logo.

   _____

5. What company uses the slogan "Think different"™ to sell its product?

   _____

6. "Did somebody say . . ."

   _____

7. "When your bank says no . . ."

   _____

8. "It's everywhere you want to be . . ."

   _____

9. "Double your pleasure, double your fun with . . ."

   _____

10. "Drivers Wanted"

   _____

Figure 3–3.

student, Karen, now looks twice at almost everything the media puts in her face. She states, "advertising creates a sort of crooked reality based primarily on appearances. If every girl isn't Cindy Crawford, she is considered inferior. However, if a guy doesn't have Cindy on his arm, he is equally inferior." My students were sensitized to the unrealistic images of both men and women as well as to their own immunity to commercial messages. This documentary will generate discussions on the language of persuasion, and the ways advertising contributes to how we define our identities. A study of advertising fosters critical thinking skills and encourages students to explore how they negotiate meaning with media texts.

Questioning Barbie and the Marlboro Man

Before we formally began the unit examining gender issues, another preliminary activity was a discussion of two of the most recognizable pop-culture icons in the media, Barbie and the Marlboro Man, and an examination of how they serve to provide us with cultural ideas of feminity and masculinity. Female students unanimously agreed on Barbie's voluptuous perfection when discussing her anatomy: long legs, long arms, long neck, small waistline, shapely breasts, and a petite nose. As children, they loved playing with Barbie, changing her clothes, and arranging romantic dates with Ken. Unlike baby dolls, Barbie represented their first idea of feminine beauty. The questions I posed were

1. What does Barbie's image reveal about our society and its values?
2. Why do we admire Barbie's anatomically challenged body?
3. How does the Barbie industry create insatiable consumerism?
4. Is Barbie a negative role model for impressionable young girls?

We stopped to remind ourselves that she's an 11½-inch doll, yet the image she's projected since 1959 has powerfully affected the coming-of-age of generations of girls.

Next, we took a look at the Marlboro Man, an image so ubiquitous that since 1954 it has advertised cigarettes more powerfully than any words could. We brainstormed what he symbolizes: freedom, rugged individuality, heroism, stoicism, and virility. We discussed how these associations reflect the values of our society. Since the company can't advertise the qualities of its product, Philip Morris manipulates consumers by creating an image that makes powerful cultural associations. The Marlboro Man projects a state of mind, a lifestyle, a physique—all of which reflect an image of how our society perceives masculinity. Stimulated by these discussions, we were ready to explore broader gender issues in advertising.

Exploring Gender in Advertisements
A Group Activity

In order to explore gender issues and to develop a framework for critically viewing the media, I asked my students to find print ads from magazines and newspapers that either reinforce or challenge gender stereotypes. Our goal was to analyze and evaluate these visual images in order to recognize the persuasive power of these representations on our values and attitudes. Advertising is an accessible medium for exploring complex gender issues regarding idealized looks, cultural stereotypes, and consumerism.

I arranged the class into small groups whose task it was to examine the ads the students had brought to class. One person was designated to record the observations of the group. Guided viewing questions included:

- What product is being advertised?
- How are the men and women portrayed?
- What traits are desirable for men and women, as evident in these ads?
- Do men and women really look like those represented in advertising?
- Do these ads reinforce gender stereotypes?
- Are women shown in traditional roles?
- Are they sexually objectified?
- Do these ads challenge gender stereotypes?
- Are men shown nurturing children or in domestic roles?
- How do these ads play on our anxieties, doubts, and fears?
- Do these ads promote gender equality?

Through interaction in peer groups, students discover, together, that each ad contains a subtext or an implicit meaning, that is not readily apparent to a casual observer. Some of the subtexts that students discovered showed their excellent analytical skills. One group observed that designer clothing ads sell men and women the "gospel according to Tommy Hilfiger, Ralph Lauren, and Calvin Klein." These "prophets" reinforce gender stereotypes, and "preach" looks and lifestyles to the masses who accept their messages without question. Another group raised the issue of the disturbing subtext of soft-core pornography in advertising. Do Victoria's Secret lingerie ads have the power to excite lascivious behavior? Does an ad for Jordache jeans equate sex with power and violence? A third group particularly enjoyed deconstructing an ad for Tampax. Featured quite prominently on the page in red, white, and blue graphics was a proud portrait of Rosie the Riveter with her shirtsleeve rolled up to reveal a tattoo stamped on her arm, which said, "Tampax was there." The headline read, "We can do it." The ad is an entire cultural literacy quiz in itself! During WWII, women had to work in the factories while the men were overseas to keep the economy healthy. Women performing hard work was valued in society in the 1940s. The ad clearly challenges gender stereotypes by showing a woman who, despite her monthly menstrual cycle, is quite capable of quality performance in the workplace. This woman clearly takes pride in her work.

In the 1990s, it appears that images of men in advertising are showing more of a realistic balance between traditional and nontraditional gender roles. On the one hand, masculinity is still clearly desirable. Ads for watches are endorsed by Pierce

Brosnan, who stars as James Bond, and Polo Sport cologne features a well-toned, virile Tyson Beckford. On the other hand, we discovered just as many ads that challenge stereotypical macho images. Most prevalent are those portraying nurturing men as romantic father figures. Eternity cologne captures intimate, loving images of fathers and sons. An ad for Quorum cologne bears the headline "success is knowing which appointments to keep" and features an attractive yuppie in a pinstriped suit carrying an adorable baby (holding a silver rattle) in a knapsack. Men are shown living an idealized life, with a lucrative career, a family, and financial security. However, my students and I question whether these improved images of men contribute to new inadequacies and anxieties. What pressures does advertising create so that we can "have it all"? In other ads, men's bodies are objectified and dehumanized as sex objects, as women's have often been portrayed historically. Calvin Klein's Obsession cologne ads and his underwear ads feature cropped torsos and headless prone bodies. Since the 1980s, Bruce Weber's photographs have become trademarks for the company. They feature "beefcakes," on billboards, in magazine catalogues, and on TV. Tall, attractive, bronzed young men pose seductively in their underwear. The subtext is more complex. The public accepts these passive images, which at one time were assigned exclusively to women posing in their lingerie. Weber creates shocking, provocative fantasies of objectified males who are valued for their looks. Is this what we mean by gender equality?

Clearly, the media continues to pull our social consciousness in many directions. Advertising manipulates our needs, our longings, and our insecurities. As Chrissy concluded, "we are never going to be able to measure up to the ideals before us, but the more aware we become, the less prone we are to believe these lies, and the more likely we will be to develop a sense of self-worth not derived from the perfect models we are taught to accept as real." There is no doubt that examining gender issues in advertising will raise our students' consciousness, and they will continue to analyze, question, and evaluate the bombardment of images in their daily lives long after this unit is over.

The Representation of Minority Groups in the Media

"If a child grows up seeing minorities on television as they exist in reality, she will less likely become racist and more apt to accept people's differences. Possibly, we are slowly making strides against racism in society, and the media is just catching up." Amy's optimism is shared by many of her classmates, who believe that the media has the power to help promote social change.

Although classroom teachers are forever beseiged with core curriculum requirements, not one of us can afford to ignore the complexities of the culture in which we live. In 1999, an epidemic of hate crimes infected society. Black actor Danny Glover couldn't get a cab to stop for him in Manhattan. James Byrd was dragged three miles to his death down a road in rural Texas by three white supremacists. College student

Matthew Shepard was beaten, tied to a post, and left to die because he was gay. Buford Furrow Jr., a member of Aryan Nation, murdered a Filipino mailman and opened fire on Jewish kindergarten students. In our battle against hate, not only do we need to expand laws to protect Blacks, Hispanics, Asians, Jews, gays, and the disabled, but it is imperative that we implement the policies that our state Departments of Education disseminate to local districts. In my district, we have an Equal Education Opportunity Statement, which ensures equivalency of educational opportunity throughout the district. Specifically, it mandates that our school district's curricula will "eliminate discrimination, promote mutual acceptance and respect among students, and enable students to interact effectively with each other regardless of race, national origin, gender, religion, English proficiency, socioeconomic status, sexual orientation, or ability level." Examining the representation of gender, race, and marginal groups will heighten student awareness of the way in which the media reflects the complexities of contemporary culture and affects the way we view others.

Educational goals throughout many districts in the country infuse multiculturalism into existing curricula. Media literacy can be used as a vehicle to foster critical viewing and tolerance in the lives of our students. Sadly, the media has constructed a reality that is often a distortion or a misrepresentation of life in America. Racial groups are often underrepresented, stereotyped, or invisible.

A recent article in the *New York Times* (20 September 1999) by Bernard Weinraub, titled "Stung by Criticism of the New Fall Shows, TV Networks Rush to Add Minority Groups," addresses a timely media issue. How is television responding to the need for multicultural representation? In the fall 1999 season, Black, Latino, and Asian groups voiced strong criticism on the lack of non-Whites in this season's lineup. There has been a rush to add minority roles to redress the underrepresentation; however, this is not enough, according to the members of these groups. An entire mind-set must change in the attitudes of network executives, producers, and advertisers. According to actor James McDaniel, "People running television live on the mean streets of Malibu, and minorities just don't exist in their world." Kweisi Mfume, president of the NAACP, made an aggressive move by purchasing one hundred shares in each of the companies that own CBS, NBC, ABC, and Fox "so we can go to board meetings and raise the kind of hell and the kind of issues that we think are necessary." Obviously, representation means more than hiring black actors and writers. It means that minorities should be hired in decision-making roles. According to Weinraub, it appears that "the failure to reach beyond all white casts is not the result of overt racism, but more indifference and insensitivity on the part of the networks." My students were disturbed by several issues in this article. Dana said, "it shouldn't be a difficult task for writers to include all different types of people, because this country is composed of myriad people, not just Whites." Jordana raised the issue of tokenism in the article. "By simply throwing in a minority to any given part does not solve the problem. In a way, it makes things worse . . . the writers of these shows can make a difference by creating leading parts for minorities in the script." Most students agreed that the rush to add minority characters is more a symbolic gesture to appease the

NAACP than a new direction for the industry. Bringing current media issues in the news into the classroom is guaranteed to stimulate lively discussion as well as thoughtful writing.

Viewing Color Adjustment *with Students*

In order to give my students a historical perspective of minority representation in the media, we viewed Marlon Riggs' provocative documentary, *Color Adjustment* (1991), which traces race relations for over forty years through the lens of prime-time entertainment. The documentary opens with Ruby Dee's mellifluous voice narrating, "This is the American dream." The images on the screen show Ozzie, Harriet, David, and Ricky Nelson. Then she says, "This is a picture of what the dream has become." We next see the Cosby and Jefferson families. Although "color" has been "adjusted" on TV over the past fifty years, the representation of minorities continues to be a sensitive issue. Students have little or no understanding of how the media has dealt with race. They must be educated in order to understand the relationship between images in the media and race relations in this country.

Color Adjustment provides a historic context that traces the representation of Blacks, from the postwar era to the 1980s. After WWII, Blacks who had fought in the first integrated troops returned to this country with a "cautious optimism." Although they had fought for the freedom of others and were ready to be integrated into American society, they were denied equality in this country. Television, which was in its technological infancy, continued to air such successful radio formats as dramas, westerns, and comedies. One of the most successful radio comedies was *Amos and Andy*, in which two white actors, Gosden and Correll, impersonated the black characters. However, when the show moved to television in 1951, it had an all-black cast and enjoyed enormous popularity. Unfortunately, in its efforts to entertain, it reinforced negative stereotypes and cliches of black people. Although the war had transformed the role of Blacks in society, they were represented by images on TV that continued to show them in a separate community. Fifty years later, the controversy still exists. The majority of my students had never even heard of *Amos and Andy*. The documentary provides enough clips for the students to make up their own minds regarding this controversy. Jordana commented, "The popular show used typical stereotypes of African Americans to please the audience. This is completely unfair to Blacks to be ridiculed and patronized over national television. For most Americans who did not know any better, their perceptions of the black race were formed by what the show depicted." Michael was shocked by the discussion and exclaimed, "I can't believe how narrow-minded white America was back in the fifties. After WWII, African Americans who had fought in the war expected to come back to an integrated America. However, they came back to the same segregation they experienced before the war."

TV shows such as *The Beulah Show* (1950) and *Amos and Andy* (1951) stereotyped Blacks as uneducated and serving as maids. It was only when *The Nat King Cole Show* (1956) appeared that there was finally a sophisticated, charming, genteel, and talented Black on TV. Sadly, this popular show was canceled after one season—the show lacked sponsors who didn't want to alienate southern audiences. The documentary continues to trace race relations with *Julia* (1968), *All in the Family* (1970), and *The Cosby Show* (1984). At the end of the documentary, my students were generally shocked, disgusted, and amazed, but still thinking about the unfair treatment of minorities on TV and how they continue to struggle to gain the acceptance they deserve fifty years later. Nikki says, "After watching the documentary and sharing opinions in class discussions about such serious topics, the only way to describe my feelings is shock and utter disbelief. My reaction is not totally aimed at the producers, writers, and advertising agencies,who so ignorantly failed to include minorities, but at myself for being so blind to an almost all-white medium."

The Latin Beat

I had spent quite a bit of time discussing my unit on the representation of Latinos in the media with a colleague of mine from the foreign language department. Instead of continuing our conversations in the hall, I invited her and her student teacher to join us on the day we viewed excerpts from a documentary aired on ABC in October 1999 titled *The Latin Beat*. Once again, I raised the question of how representation, in this case of Latinos, affects our attitudes of others. Although there are fifteen million Latinos in the United States, images of them in prime-time TV and films are generally underrepresented and reinforce negative stereotypes. Men are often typecast in the roles of gang members, outlaws, or criminals, while women are portrayed as sex objects. The general attitude of Latino actors has been to "take what's available." Selma Hayek knows about rejection. In the documentary, she relates an anecdote about not being cast as a scientist because she's Mexican. At one point in her career, she was encouraged to emphasize the Lebanese side of her family rather than the Mexican. Several male actors, however, such as Edward James Olmos, Jimmy Smits, Andy Garcia, and Antonio Bandaras, have enjoyed professional success. And women such as Gloria Estefan, Jennifer Lopez, and Cameron Diaz carry on the legacy of such Latina talents as Rita Moreno and Chita Rivera.

My students were familiar only with Latinos represented in the music industry, which has proven to be the most commercially successful arena for their culture. Author Guy Garcia, in his article titled "Another Latin Boom, But Different," (*New York Times*, 27 June 1999, 25–27) states, "Latinos have arrived and the whole world is listening." With the success of Jennifer Lopez, Ricky Martin, and Marc Anthony, Latin music has been accepted into the mainstream of popular music. Tommy Mottola, chairman of Sony Music Entertainment, says, "This craze, this phenomenon is not exactly new to us; it's just that everybody's catching on to it, recognizing it and jumping on the bandwagon." Latino entertainers have crossed over into popular mainstream culture before. Xavier Cugat, Desi Arnaz, Carmen Miranda, Richie Valens, and Carlos Santana have all been successful, but their impact has not lasted. The Latino music market has been growing, and Americans are embracing the cross-cultural appeal of Latin performers.

Nickelodeon has a new program slated for the 2000 season titled *Taina*, which is targeted for teenagers and their parents and which deals with universal themes as they aply to a teenager, her multicultural family, and her friends. Most of the major roles will be played by Latino actors, a rarity today. Nickelodeon is responding to the demographic growth of Latinos in the United States and the network's commitment to reflect society realistically. Maria Perez-Brown, the show's producer and creator, said in a recent *New York Times* article that she wrote *Taina* keeping in mind the influence television has in shaping the attitudes and self-esteem of children. "This girl is going to be true to herself. She's going to know who she is and not feel inferior. Nothing is going to stop this girl from pursuing success in her own terms" ("Nickelodeon Discovers a Large New World to Portray," *New York Times*, 1 November 1999, E1). Isn't this the profile we'd like to see for all of our students? Portraying strong, independent, self-confident teenagers on TV is a positive way for television to have an impact on young people today.

Student Project

To evaluate learning in this unit, I use an authentic assessment. Media literacy not only fosters comprehension and interpretation of media messages, but also empowers students to produce their own messages. I ask my students to reflect on the issue of representation in the media. What do they notice now that they never noticed before? Have their views regarding advertising, television, music, and film changed? The assignment asks students to become actively involved in the process of creating an original advertising campaign or a public service announcement for a product or cause that currently exists and that reflects their experience of this unit. This assessment fosters critical thinking skills and offers an opportunity to accommodate different learning styles.

Students must think about an image they want to convey and whether they will address gender, race, marginal groups, or any combination of these issues. Will they reinforce or challenge cultural stereotypes? I encourage them to create campaigns that are meaningful, sensitive, and interpretive. Each campaign has two components: a visual display and a formal essay. The visual display is an 8½-by-11-inch presentation that resembles a page in a magazine. They may use magazine cutouts, photographs, or computer images. In addition, they must compose informative, engaging copy to convey their message, using headlines, slogans, and manipulative techniques of commercial advertising including testimonial, bandwagon, transfer, hidden fears, word magic, and so on (see Figure 3–1). I remind my students that the product itself is not what's important in this campaign. Rather, it's the image or the message that will ultimately "sell" the product. In the essay, they must defend their campaigns, discussing the techniques and creative choices they've made such as the representation of images, the language, the layout, and the emotional appeal. The conclusion should be a statement about the direction of advertising in the new millennium. In her media journal, Blake expressed the following response: "We hardly ever get a chance to show our creativity and our own interpretation of what we have learned. We are constantly bombarded by objective tests that require us to record our answers on Scantron sheets that only show that we are effective memorizers." Blake's campaign was a public service announcement urging women to vote, and she used Susan B. Anthony and Elizabeth Cady Stanton as testimonials. In his multicultural ad for Banana Republic, Michael used the slogan "Human Being Being Human" to create emotional appeal. His ad campaign is focused toward breaking stereotypes of beautiful Caucasian people that he feels the media represents. He is not only selling clothing in his ad, but youth, fun, sophistication, and style. In his search for pictures of young people of different races, he couldn't find any Latino or Native American models, so he wound up taking photographs of his friends. Michael states, "the last two weeks in class and creating my own ad have been an enlightening experience. I realized that minorities are not equally represented in ads, and they should be since they do make up the mass of consumers. They should be represented in a respectful, tasteful way, and not just thrown is as a form of tokenism." Jackie also finds tokenism to be offensive, and chose to create a public service announcement for cancer awareness that addresses different genders and racial and age groups to suggest that cancer can strike anyone. Her slogan was "One World, One Cause," implying that we are all in this together because cancer doesn't discriminate, and we must try to stop this disease together. In the future, Jackie believes that "ads will have to become more sensitive to cultural groups." Jordana chose to advertise the New York Marathon as a race for everyone, "a gathering of spirit for the city." Her ad, which is a collage of faces, symbolizes "unity between races, ethnic groups, and genders." It challenges cultural stereotypes and includes images of a Hispanic man playing cricket, an Asian woman leading an aerobics class, a Caucasian female playing football, and an elderly man running. Jordana's hope for advertising in the future is that it will challenge all prejudices and stereotypes and not simply include minorities out of pity, but rather out of a desire to teach future generations that although everyone is different on the outside, we are all human on the inside. In her research for her campaign for Fuji film, Amanda had to look in *National Geographic* to find diverse photographs because it was impossible to find them in *People* magazine. She believes that if the representation of people remains the same as we enter the millennium, our society "should be ashamed that we base everything on the color of your skin and physical appearance." She hopes the future will be bright and we "fight against the superficial images that the advertising industry places in our lives." Seth truly addresses the heart of the assignment in his ad campaign for Nike. His ad features a young African American boy wearing a knit cap bearing the Nike "swoosh." The copy reads, "I Like Nike, too." Seth's opinion is that most advertisers overlook minority groups. His campaign conveys a "desperate attempt at inclusion of the African American child into the mainstream of the Nike vision. This vision of universal opportunity, benefits of hard work, and active participation in life speaks beyond merely selling sneakers and represents the American dream." Seth's ad appeals to Nike to let this child into its club, while at the same time making a broader plea to all of America for inclusion, equality, acceptance, and respect for different cultures. In his simple ad with a single line of copy, Seth addresses several of the most pressing social issues of our age. His campaign, as well as the other student responses, shows evidence of sensitivity to the problems of representation in the media. Not only have my students met the requirements of the assignment, but also the mandates of the Equal Education Opportunity Statement, as they have produced original media messages reflecting a high level of abstract thinking in a creative way.

In his article in the *New York Times* (26 September 1999) titled "What's So Bad About Hate?" Andre Sullivan maintains, "a free country will always mean a hateful country. This may not be fair, or perfect, or admirable, but it is reality, and while we need not endorse it, we should not delude ourselves into thinking we can prevent it." In the aftermath of Columbine, I believe we as educators are obligated to sensitize our students to sexism, racism, and anti-Semitism and to help promote diversity, harmony, inclusion, acceptance, and respect for different cultures and lifestyles. Unless these goals are met, our core curriculum standards will fall short of what is truly essential about public education, and living in a democracy.

Writing Assignments

ADVERTISING

1. Respond to Jean Kilbourne's statement in the documentary *Still Killing Us Softly I* (1987): "There are tremendous penalties for women who don't conform to culturally accepted standards of beauty."

2. Comment on this statement by Dr. Mary Pipher, author of *Reviving Ophelia* (1994): "Girls compare their own bodies to our cultural ideals and find them wanting . . . girls developed eating disorders when our culture developed a standard of beauty that they couldn't obtain by being healthy."

3. Do you envision a time when people can move beyond being "masculine" or "feminine" or African American, Asian American, Latino, or physically challenged to simply being human?

4. Reflecting on gender issues in advertising, comment on the following statement: "Advertising isn't so much about selling a product as it is about marketing insecurity."

5. Images of men in the 1950s have changed in the 1990s. How would you define the male ideal as we enter the millennium?

6. Pornography reduces women to objects and takes away their humanity. Ads sometimes remove women's individuality by portraying them in dismembered parts, showing headless torsos, legs, hands, breasts, buttocks. How do you feel about the objectification of women in advertising? What is the psychological effect? How might the negative images affect how women are treated in American culture? Sexist advertising techniques used against women are also used to objectify men. Men, too, are dehumanized. How do you feel about the role reversals?

7. If images of men and women in advertising communicated a full range of humanness by race, age, size, and physical ability, and did not reinforce gender stereotypes, would they still "sell" products and services effectively? Do consumers want reality in advertising?

8. Design an ad campaign using the theme: "Beauty isn't about looking young."

9. Find ads from newspapers and magazines that prey upon the fears and insecurities of consumers. Discuss these messages.

10. Find ads that might be considered "soft porn." Describe why you feel this way.

11. Find ads that contribute to eating disorders. Explain their power.

12. Leaf through issues of *G.Q.*, *Esquire*, and *Details*. Are these magazines the masculine versions of *Cosmopolitan*? Point to specific ads, articles, and gender issues. Discuss your views.

13. Examine Calvin Klein Obsession and underwear ads. Contrast them to ads for Eternity cologne for men. What do you notice about the different representations of men?

TELEVISION

1. What groups do you fit into in society (gender, age, religion, family, race, nationality, socioeconomic)? Discuss the television shows that best reflect your groups.

2. In your own television viewing, have you "crossed the color line"? Do you watch shows featuring Whites and Blacks not distinguishing racial differences? Is your viewing "colorblind"? What criteria do you use to determine what you watch?

3. Unlike the major networks, NBC, CBS, or ABC, independent networks such as Fox, WB, and UPN feature many sitcoms with all black casts such as *Moesha*, *Martin*, and *Sister Sister*. Do any of these popular shows promote derogatory stereotypes? Contrast these shows to shows with well-integrated casts such as *N.Y.P.D. Blue*, *ER*, and *Law and Order*.

4. Compare and contrast the representation of the American family in the 1950s and the 1990s.

5. Watch reruns of *All in the Family*. Was Archie Bunker a racist? Why would Norman Lear create such a prime-time character? Research the social climate of the 1970s. Can television be a vehicle for social change?

6. Compare and contrast the representation of single working-women as portrayed by *Mary Tyler Moore* in the 1970s and *Ally McBeal* in the 1990s.

7. View vintage shows featuring women: Lucy, June Cleaver, Alice Cramden, Harriet Nelson, Donna Stone, Mary Tyler Moore. How have the roles of women changed? Contrast these women to women featured on television today.

8. View shows, such as *Dawson's Creek*, featuring gay characters. Do these portrayals challenge or reinforce stereotypes?

9. Controversy is good marketing. Research *The Murphy Brown Show* and former vice president Dan Quayle's complaint that the program showed no regard for family values. Research the barrage of publicity that became a national event when Ellen Degeneres "came out."

FILM

1. Compare and contrast the portrayal of race in Rob Reiner's *Ghosts of Mississippi* to the real story of the assassination of Medgar Evers. Investigate Spike Lee's representation of Malcolm X in his film and compare it to the real Malcom X.

2. Spike Lee is very concerned with the way Blacks are represented on screen. View *Crooklyn*. How is the African American family represented? *Jungle Fever* is the story of an interracial love affair. What is disturbing about this film? *Do the Right Thing* powerfully represents minorities, gender, and age. What message is Lee imparting to his audience about the themes of violence and tolerance?

3. Discuss the role of race as it is portrayed by Rod Steiger and Sidney Poitier in the film *In the Heat of the Night*.

4. Compare and contrast the portrayal of Hispanics in *Ma Familia* and *El Norte*.

5. Watch *West Side Story*. Does the film reinforce negative cultural stereotypes or is it a realistic representation of Puerto Ricans in the 1950s?

6. Investigate the casting problems in making the film *The Joy Luck Club*. Read the novel by Amy Tan, and discuss the differences between female Asian immigrants and their American-born daughters.

Viewing Assignments

TELEVISION

1. Watch reruns of *All in the Family*. Identify the issues that "blew the lid off" network television in the 1970s. Why was this show heralded as groundbreaking?

2. Watch *Moesha*. How does the show represent a middle-class African American family coping with the same problems millions of American confront every day?

3. How do the following shows represent gender, minorities, elderly, and gays? Do the characters challenge or reinforce stereotypes?

Friends, Dharma and Greg, Ally McBeal, Seinfeld	(gender)
Boston Public, ER, N.Y.P.D. Blue, Law and Order, The West Wing	(minorities)
The Golden Girls	(elderly)
Will and Grace, Dawson's Creek	(gays)

4. Select a profession. View a show that reveals that profession. How is it represented? Realistically? Stereotypically? Sensitively? Humorously?
Law: *Ally McBeal, Law and Order, The Practice, Judging Amy*
Medicine: *ER, Gideon's Crossing, Third Watch*
Law Enforcement: *N.Y.P.D. Blue, Law and Order, Judging Amy*
Media: *Sports Night, Suddenly Susan*
Politics: *The West Wing, Spin City*

5. Does art imitate life on television? Find examples of shows that exhibit social realism. For example, how are single-parent families represented?

6. What is the relationship between media and society? What can you learn about an era in which a show was created? *Father Knows Best* ('50s), *The Dick Van Dyke Show* ('60s), *All in the Family* ('70s), *The Cosby Show* ('80s), *Seinfeld* ('90s).

FILM

1. Many different roles for women are featured in films. Describe the traits of "real" women and contrast them to the traits of "media" women. Do films challenge or reinforce gender stereotypes?
Silence of the Lambs (Jodie Foster plays an F.B.I. agent)
The Accused (Kelly McGillis plays a lawyer)
The China Syndrome (Jane Fonda plays a TV news reporter)
Broadcast News (Holly Hunter plays a TV news producer)
Norma Rae (Sally Fields plays a labor organizer)
Thelma and Louise (Susan Sarandon and Geena Davis play housewives)

2. Examine films that reinforce male stereotypes, such as the physically invincible, sexually irresistible roles played by Sylvester Stallone, Arnold Schwarzenegger, and Steven Seagal. Or the loner played by Harrison Ford or Clint Eastwood. Or the emotionally well-balanced nice guy played by Tom Hanks. How do these roles reflect our culture?

3. Watch the scene in Spike Lee's film *Do the Right Thing*, which is a montage of racial epithets. Why would a filmmaker use such abusive statements against minority groups?

4. Film exposes audiences to those who are different. Sometimes images contribute to misconceptions about others, and sometimes they don't. Viewers should be sensitized to marginal groups such as the mentally impaired (*What's Eating Gilbert Grape, Rainman*), the physically impaired (*My Left Foot, The Elephant Man, Coming Home, Born on the 4th of July, Awakenings, Places in the Heart, Children of a Lesser God, Mask, Niagara, Niagara*), the elderly (*On Golden Pond, Cocoon, Driving Miss Daisy, Nobody's Fool, The Trip to Bountiful*), gays (*Torch Song Trilogy, Gods and Monsters*) the overweight (*What's Eating Gilbert Grape*), and Native Americans (*Dances with Wolves, Smoke Signals*). What is the value of these films?

5. Teenagers of diverse racial backgrounds have been dramatically represented in films. What do we learn about African American and Hispanic cultures in such films as *Boyz in the Hood*, *Higher Learning*, *Dangerous Minds*, *Stand and Deliver*, and *Do the Right Thing*? Do films have the power to change misconceptions of the individuals that make up minority groups?

6. *Smoke Signals* (1998) is the first feature-length movie to be written, directed, and acted by Native Americans. It's all about self-representation. Watching this film, what do you learn about the culture? How does the film explore identity without resorting to Hollywood cliches?

7. Professions are represented in film as they are on television. Watch a film featuring a profession, such as teaching in *Stand and Deliver* or *The Dead Poets Society*, and then interview a teacher in your school. What is real about the representation and what is constructed? Other professions might include journalism in *All the Presidents Men* or *Absence of Malice*, scientists in *Contact*, or lawyers in *Ghosts of Mississippi*.

Cultural Literacy Quiz 1 Answer Key

1. L; 2. X; 3. R; 4. G; 5. O; 6. Q; 7. M; 8. T; 9. N; 10. S; 11. V; 12. A; 13. U; 14. C; 15. J; 16. F; 17. H; 18. B; 19. W; 20. P; 21. D; 22. I; 23. K; 24. E.

Cultural Literacy Quiz 2 Answer Key

1. swing, country western; 2. Serena and Venus Williams; 3. Absolut; 4. Just do it/Swoosh; 5. Apple computers; 6. Toyota; 7. Champion says yes; 8. Visa; 9. Doublemint gum; 10. VW.

Videos Cited

The Ad and the Ego, 1996, Harold Boihem, California Newsreel, 57 min.

Color Adjustment, 1991, Marlon Riggs, California Newsreel, 87 min.

The Latin Beat, 1999, ABC Television, 60 min.

Still Killing Us Softly, 1987, Cambridge Documentary Films, Inc., 32 min.

Works Cited

GARCIA, GUY. "Another Latin Boom, But Different." *New York Times* 27 June 1999: 25–27.

HIRSCH, JR., ED, JOSEPH F. KETT, AND JAMES TREFIL. 1993. *The Dictionary of Cultural Literacy*. New York: Houghton Mifflin.

NAVARRO, MIREYA. "Nickelodeon Discovers a Large New World to Portray." *New York Times* 1 November 1999: E, 1:4.

NICHOLSON, JENNIFER. 1992. "The Advertiser's Man." *AD Busters* 20–26.

PIPHER, MARY M. D. 1994. *Reviving Ophelia*. New York: Ballantine Books.

SULLIVAN, ANDREW. "What's So Bad About Hate?" *New York Times* 26 September 1999: 50.

TWITCHELL, JAMES. 1996. *Ad Cult USA: The Triumph of Advertising in American Culture*. New York: Columbia University Press.

WEINRAUB, BERNARD. "Stung by Criticism of the New Fall Shows, TV Networks Rush to Add Minority Groups." *New York Times* 20 September 1999 A, 1:1.

FOUR

Analyzing the Moving Image: Basic Terminology

MARY T. CHRISTEL

For the most part, when teachers develop strategies to discuss a film in the English classroom they primarily focus on a film's narrative structure: plot, character, theme. The elements of film that are most similar to literature are familiar and comfortable elements to discuss. Unfortunately, examining just the narrative qualities of a film ignores what makes film unique—it moves. It has a kinetic vitality that is not duplicated in any other visual art form. To best understand how to analyze a moving image, the viewer must understand not only the different levels of movement integrated into a single sequence but also the levels of sound integrated into that image to further enhance its dynamic qualities.

In Chapter 1 we discussed visual composition as it applies to the analysis of single, static images. The five principles of visual composition defined there (arrangement, placement, framing, lighting, and color) certainly come to bear on the analysis of moving images as well. We need to remember that moving images are simply twenty-four frames of still pictures running through a projector each second to create movement.

The Basics

The best place to start in order to develop a vocabulary to discuss cinematic techniques of camera movement, editing, and sound is Pyramid Films' *Basic Film Terms: A Visual Dictionary*. While dated in its visual style there is no better short film to quickly illustrate the most basic techniques through visual examples and succinct voice-over narration.

To supplement the five principles of visual composition, it is necessary to add the following terms, which further define the different kinds of shots and specific elements contained within the single shot.

shot	the single image captured by running film through a camera and turning it on, then off; individual shots must be joined together (edited) to form a sequence (series of shots)
take	synonym for shot
camera angle	the degree to which the camera is looking up or down at the subject in the shot
one-shot	one figure/person in shot
two-shot	two figures/people in shot
close-up	human face or object is dominant element in shot; no environmental or situational context to shot
medium shot	torso of human figure is dominant element in shot, less environmental or situational context to shot
long shot	human figure, subject shown in context of its environment
establishing shot	long shot that reveals location, context of scene
bird's-eye view	extreme high-angle shot that takes in the view of the location and dwarfs and distorts figures in shot
reaction shot	one-shot that reveals character's expression
shot/reverse shot	one-shot cuts between two characters interacting with one another
eyeline match	cut between one-shot of character looking at a specific point to what he is seeing

Obviously these terms complement the terms defined and discussed in Chapter 1, and students will need to see how these components work in the context of actual film footage. Volume 2 of *The Art of Film* series, "The Camera," is useful to screen as a supplement to *Basic Film Terms* and visual composition strategies to reinforce the basic elements of camera placement and use. However, one technique from Chapter 1, lighting, deserves expanded treatment here.

Lighting   *know difference b/tw key*

Lighting is a technique that is very easy to take for granted, but it is crucial to the development of a concept known as *mise-en-scene*. Simply understood, mise-en-scene refers to the visual style of a film, and some directors cultivate their own visual signature on their films over their entire career. Mise-en-scene, as defined by Bordwell and Thompson in *Film Art* (1986), includes setting, costume, makeup, figure movement, and lighting. Lighting adds tremendously to mood and tone in visual

Know the differences

images and directs the viewer's eye to crucial elements within a shot. A more expanded vocabulary from Chapter 1 to discuss lighting techniques includes the following terms:

key light	main light source in a given shot
floodlight	casts wide expanses of light
spotlight	accentuates a particular figure or element in a shot
back lighting	light source is behind subject in shot, creates glow or halo
diffused light	light beam generally altered by smoke, fog, or mist
pin spot	highly concentrated beams of light, usually eerie in its effect
shadow	the absence of light

The final term listed may seem unusual in a list of terms that apply to lighting techniques, but the absence of light can be as powerful as the absence of sound. The film that best, and most provocatively, used the absence of light or shadow is Orson Welles' *Citizen Kane*. The reporter, Thompson, is literally enveloped in darkness for the entire film. That technique works metaphorically, since Thompson is "in the dark" until the very end of the film when he finally discovers the meaning of "Rosebud." In John Ford's film *Stagecoach*, the climactic shootout takes place at night, and Ford manipulates what the viewer is able to see and not see to maximize the suspense in a scene that even by 1939 was well worn in the standard "high noon" treatment of this situation. Lighting, therefore, has a tremendous impact on film style.

Subject Movement and Film Speed

The earliest filmmakers kept their cameras in a fixed position and relied on subject movement to provide the visual interest for a particular subject or event. Thomas Edison's earliest thirty-second kinetoscope peepshow reels featured a man sneezing, exotic dancers strutting their stuff, and a muscle man flexing his pecs. As cinema developed as an art form, the content of individual shots became more complex, but the importance of subject movement certainly has not diminished. Subject movement can be positioned in the foreground, middle ground, or background. A subject can move toward or away from the camera at varying rates of speed and in varying combinations. Another aspect of film movement is the manipulation of film speed. Directors and editors can *undercrank* (speed up) or *overcrank* (slow down) a sequence to alter the duration of the shot on the scene as well as to manipulate subject movement.

Actually screening early silent films for students who have never carefully analyzed the moving image is a great place to begin. These films move slowly and employ basic visual composition, editing, and narrative techniques. Edwin S. Porter's *The*

Great Train Robbery develops a realistic narrative that includes dramatic close-ups, the first pan shot, crude tracking, and crosscutting (these terms are defined below). In terms of subject movement, Porter is one of the first directors to explore having simultaneous action occurring in the foreground, middle ground, and background. George Melies' *A Trip to the Moon* offers an early example of a science fiction film. He bases his narrative on the Jules Verne story. He innovates trick photography that gives the illusions of people and things appearing and disappearing and uses crude dissolves and superimpositions. Influenced by his theatrical background, Melies' subject movement is carefully choreographed or blocked. Both of these films are available in *The Movies Begin* series.

Camera Movement   *Know differences*

The ability of the camera to move greatly enhances the dynamic quality of an image or subject whether it is moving or not. There are a few basic ways that the camera can move:

tracking	camera follows subject horizontally through space, usually on wheels set into a track or mounted on a vehicle; also called dollying
fluid camera	tracking that follows subject for an extended period of time
pan	camera follows subject horizontally (back and forth) on a fixed based such as a tripod
tilt	camera, mounted on tripod, moves move up or down from a fixed base
crane	camera is lifted vertically through space to follow its subject from a bird's-eye view to a close-up or vice versa; also called boom

The most dynamic forms of camera movement shots are the tracking and crane shots, since they tend to cover the most physical space.

Camera movement can also be achieved and enhanced through the use of a special lens. Instead of tracking, a camera can move from a long shot to a close-up through the use of a *zoom* lens, which unlike the tracking shot keeps all the planes in focus. A staple of the suspense genre is the *rack focus* shot, which brings an element of the shot in, say, the foreground, clearly into focus and then moves that element out of focus and brings another aspect of the shot into focus. For example, a student sitting at her desk busy at work is in focus in the foreground of the shot. In the background of the shot another student is peering over her shoulder. To get a better view of the student peering over the girl's shoulder, the camera shifts focus from the girl in the foreground to the second student in the background. With these techniques, the camera creates the illusion of movement.

Editing

The most unique aspect of film is its ability to place two images side by side. Those images can be selected and combined to create a high level of visual continuity or they can be juxtaposed to create visual contrasts. The way those images are combined can communicate different levels of information about the development of the narrative, the relationship between images, and the passage of time. The most common forms of editing are

straight cut	basic editing transition joining two shots together without any optical effect; maintains visual and narrative continuity
fade in/fade out	image moves to black and a second image emerges from black to replace first image; generally conveys passage of time
dissolve	first shot fades as a second image emerges on the screen; there is a momentary overlapping of images
crosscutting	cutting between story lines within a narrative, also known as parallel editing
matchcut	the combination of two shots that requires elements in the second shot to perfectly line up with elements in the first shot to maintain visual continuity
cutaway	shot that presents a visual detail or action within a sequence that is part of the main action

Editing techniques that provide more unusual, complex, or trick transitions are

superimposition	two images overlap and are held for an extended period of time
wipe	one image is pulled across the screen to reveal a second image
jump cut	a techniques that joins shots together but that doesn't emphasize continuity between the shot
montage	assembly of shots intended to condense or expand time or to develop a theme; or convey an idea through the complex juxtaposition of shots; rapid cutting to produce an emotional reaction in the viewer

Actually, the definition of montage given here does not provide a sufficient explanation of this highly complex technique. Thomas and Vivian Sobchack (1987) examine this editing theory in their textbook, *An Introduction to Film*, in Chapter 3 in a section titled "Meaning Through Editing—Relationships Between Shots." Especially useful in their treatment of this technique is their discussion of how shots can be joined to create visual metaphors. They present the following example of how this effect is achieved in a comic context:

> In Chaplin's *The Gold Rush* (1925), the little tramp visually changes on screen from a man into a human-size chicken through a dissolve. The tramp, shuffling his feet to keep warm, seems to his starving companion to be a chicken scratching the ground; therefore, the little tramp is a chicken in the image. (153)

Russian filmmaker Sergei Eisenstein explores creating more complex visual metaphors in *Potemkin*, which the next chapter discusses as a film to use in excerpt form to examine editing techniques. Bordwell and Thompson (1986) also offer a very useful and accessible discussion of editing in *Film Art*. Finally, Volume 5 of *The Art of Film* series offers a twenty-minute compilation of scenes from world cinema accompanied by voice-over narration to set up each clip and explain the editing techniques involved in "The Edited Image."

In addition to being able to recognize the type of editing transition and the cinematic meaning it conveys, it is also vital to examine how editing controls the pacing of a scene. If a director favors extended tracking or fluid camerawork, a single shot may last from one to five minutes. Depending upon how fast the camera moves through space or follows its subject, the pace that is created could be described as slow and sustained. If the editor combines a series of shots that are less than thirty seconds in duration, the pace of the sequence will obviously feel quicker than when using the extended tracking shot. The shower scene in Hitchcock's *Psycho* is a penultimate example of how shots move quickly across the screen to inform, disorient, and shock the viewer. In the crop-dusting scene from *North by Northwest*, the shots at the beginning of the sequence are much longer in duration to reflect Roger Thornhill's anticipation of finally meeting the elusive George Kaplan. Once the crop-dusting plane arrives to hunt him down, the shots are much shorter in duration, and the juxtaposition of shots leaves the viewer wondering where the plane is in relationship to Thornhill. A film like *The Thin Red Line* uses shots of much longer duration than normal or expected in order to focus the viewer's attention on details in nature or to reflect the tedium and anticipation of men in battle.

Point of View

A more sophisticated way to examine the role of the camera in a sequence is to determine what point of view it takes in the scene. Gerard Genette (1980) refers to this technique as "focalization" in his study, *Narrative Discourse: An Essay in Method*. Here is a modification of that theory. First of all the camera can be *neutral* in its position in a scene. It can merely record an event objectively without editorializing on the image or event. The camera can also act *subjectively* by representing what is seen through the eyes of a particular character. The camera literally becomes the eyes of one of the characters who is witnessing, or even imagining, an event. Finally, the camera can take an *authorial* position where the camera is used very deliberately and self-consciously by the director or, as a third-person intrusive point of view, to train the viewer's eye on aspects of the scene that he might not consider important or even interesting. This strategy can provide commentary on the content of the shot or create suspense. In the latter application, the viewer is given privileged information that can create suspense. Alfred Hitchcock is probably the best practitioner of this technique. In *Psycho*, the camera roves around the motel room after Marion's death and trains the viewer's eye on the $40,000 that she has stolen and wrapped in a newspaper, and then moves the viewer's eye out the window to see the Bates' home and to hear Norman reacting to all the blood he has discovered, presumably as a result of Mother's murderous rage.

Motifs

English teachers are always accused of symbol hunting their way through literature. They can apply that skill to the study of film as well. Visual motifs certainly abound in many films. They can exist simply to create visual patterns that connect time periods or events. In Barry Levinson's *Avalon*, the presence of a television set creates a means to show the influence of the media on family dynamics and the growth of technology. Gerald Mast identifies the presence of *leitmotifs* in films, which takes the concept of the visual motif to the next level (Mast and Kawin 2000, 648). The leitmotif was actually developed in music by composer Richard Wagner and may be defined as a recurring musical theme in a composition. In film, a leitmotif can be a recurring visual or verbal component that is linked to a narrative and thematic element and that clearly resonates with a symbolic quality. In *Citizen Kane*, the word "Rosebud" is spoken as Kane dies and becomes the central force in the narrative to undercover who Kane really was in life. It is also presented as a visual element: the sled that the young Kane clutches in Colorado and that is burned in the incinerator in Xanadu in one of the closing shots of the film.

Alfred Hitchcock uses objects in a slightly different fashion. The term *plastic* is often applied to this technique. Objects for Hitchcock seldom have symbolic resonance; rather, they help build suspense. In a film like *Psycho*, the bits of paper with Marion's scribbling or the $40,000 wrapped in a newspaper become essential elements to possibly unravel the mystery of what has become of Marion Crane at the Bates Motel. In *Notorious*, the camera focuses on various bottles of wine; some actually containing wine or champagne, others containing a metal ore. These objects are presented in close-up in highly authorial shots to make a usually mundane object significant. Sometimes that significance is not immediately clear. For example, in *Notorious*, there are several shots that feature a half-full cup of coffee in close-up or in the foreground. By this time in the film, the visuals and the narrative have trained the viewer to suspect something is wrong with the coffee, especially when the character who consumes that cup of coffee starts to feel ill. Later it is revealed that the coffee in those cups is poisoned. The bottles containing metal ore become a Hitchcock

MacGuffin, another way he exploits the importance of objects. A *MacGuffin* is usually the riddle or mystery that needs to solved, the something or someone that everyone is after in the narrative. Hitchcock explained this concept to French director Francois Truffaut in Truffaut's definitive published interview of the "master of suspense" (1983, 137–139). The principle of the MacGuffin could be applied to "Rosebud" in *Citizen Kane* as well as to other films. Hitchcock is certainly not the only director to exploit the importance of objects over people in a narrative, but he certainly refines this technique and makes it a vital component of his visual style.

Sound

Though films from the silent era certainly exploit the capacity of visual storytelling, sound definitely adds much to the narrative content and directorial style of any film. Sound can basically be broken down into two broad categories: *digetic* and *nondigetic*. Bordwell and Thompson define digetic sound as "voices of characters, sounds made by objects in the story, or music represented as coming from instruments in the story" and nondigetic sound as coming from "a source outside of the story," which includes music added to the soundtrack to enhance mood and to match action or an off-camera narrator (1986, 241). Other useful terms to examine film sound include

synchronous sound	sound that matches the action
asynchronous sound	sound that doesn't match action
dialogue	presence of human voice speaking text of script; the human voice can also be present in other forms as well
subjective sound	dialogue, music, or effects that are presented as originating in the mind of a particular character
sound effects	sound isolated and added to enhance auditory impression
background sound	music, talk, noise, etc., that exist under the focal source of sound
music	music can exist as an on-camera source (radio or musician playing) or off-camera source (soundtrack music)

A good example would be selecting one of the sections from Disney's *Fantasia*. Depending on students' familiarity with this film, an analysis of "The Sorcerer's Apprentice" could begin with having students listen to the musical piece and discuss the composer's intention to tell a story through the melody and orchestration. If students are unfamiliar with the sequence, they can work out their own sequence of images in narrative or storyboard form. As they view the sequence for the first time, they should be encouraged to pick out the ways the animators clearly synchronize the tempo of the music with character movement and examine the use of lush colors, expressive lighting, and the brief use of a black-and-white image to evoke the mood of the music and a shift in the narrative. Upon second viewing, students could more carefully examine the tempo, timbre, and loudness of the music that accompany the images. A follow-up could include selecting sequences from *Fantasia 2000*, particularly the surprising application of Gershwin's "Rhapsody in Blue" to examine the coordination of a musical piece that immediately conjures a narrative line or specific visual imagery.

A good way for students to appreciate the presence of sound is to screen a sequence first without sound and then with sound. An effective example could be culled from a highly visual, screwball comedy like *My Man Godfrey*. Early in the film, a sequence is set in a hotel lobby. The scene opens with two men at a bar. Then a woman walks in with a male companion and two goats, then the scene moves into a ballroom as the woman presents her goats to another man and receives instructions from him. Students should view the scene initially with the sound turned off to isolate the visual details in the scene that mark the sequence as a comedy. As students view the sequence with sound, they would then select the elements of sound (dialogue, sound effects, background sound) that escalate the humor. That humor derives in great measure from jokes contained in the dialogue between the two men in the bar, the sound effects of the goats, and the saturated background sound of the commotion in the ballroom. The scene may be amusing visually, but it is all the more hilarious when the sound is added.

Integrating Concepts into a Viewing Plan

Using Short Clips

If students are viewing a film or television episode in a standard English classroom, it is probably impractical to assume that they will be able to acquire and master all these terms and concepts in one dose. In an elective film course, the acquisition of these terms would comprise the first unit of study. In the standard classroom, it is better to examine the kinds of viewing experiences students will have over the course of a semester or a school year, then create target concepts that integrate into each experience and that build on the previous viewing experiences.

I typically start a semester or yearlong literature course with short film sequences that are organically linked to the texts that will be the focus of an opening unit. In this way the cinematic texts are a natural part of the curriculum. I always link them to some level of narrative or cinematic analysis, so when a feature-length film is introduced it will be natural for students to approach it in a similarly analytical fashion. In an Advanced Placement (AP) literature course, I typically start with short clips that address the issue of interpretation. Students are required to form an interpretation based on an initial viewing of the clip, discuss their impressions with a partner, and view the clip a second time to apply their partner's interpretation and to evaluate the strength of an alternate reading of the cinematic text. The short, avant-garde films of Maya Deren work well for this purpose ("Meshes of the Afternoon" is examined at greater length in Chapter 5), as does an excerpt from *Jacob's Ladder* or the family din-ner scene in *True Stories*. Here is an example of the guidelines that I have used in this type of interpretive activity:

Literary Interpretation: Film Sequence Analysis

- View the clip, paying close attention to its narrative and visual qualities. This clip is taken out of context and occurs about midway through the film.

First Viewing

- Summarize what actually happens in the clip.
- List the most striking images (visual impressions) from the first viewing.
- List the images that you have the hardest time interpreting.
- How would knowing more about the context from which this clip was taken help you to make better sense of it?

Sharing with a Partner

- List the common elements of the clip that you found striking.
- List the common elements of the clip that you found problematic.
- List at least three ways that you and your partner interpreted the narrative or visual elements differently. What accounts for the differences?
- What would be the best strategies to apply to analyze the clip in order to arrive at the most accurate interpretation?

It is always optimal to select a sequence that is both visually and auditorially rich and enigmatic to focus students' attention away from analyzing just the narrative qualities that they are accustomed to examining. With advanced-level students, I start to inte-grate terms related to camera position and visual composition as we discuss their responses.

Film clips can also provide an efficient and effective way to introduce a concept or an approach that will form a connecting thread in a literature unit. Prior to intro-ducing a novel about Native Americans, James Welch's *Fools Crow*, I have screened three sequences from films that depict this racial group in three different ways to illus-trate the stereotypes that are created in popular films and literature. To illustrate the "noble savage" I have selected clips from *The Last of the Mohicans*; for "the brutal sav-age," *The Searchers*; and for the "comic savage," Disney's animated version of *Peter Pan*, especially the musical number "Why Is the Red Man Red?" For each clip the stu-dents are directed to note what the Native American character is doing, how he inter-acts with the environment and/or the other people within the scene, what kinds of emotions the focal character either expresses or withholds, and how convincing the physical representation of the Native American is (considering in the first two clips these characters are portrayed by Caucasian actors and the third clip uses an artist's conception). A second viewing of the clips would include attention to the relationship of the camera to the presentation of the main character. After discussing these three clips, I follow with a clip, possibly a more extended scene or scenes, from *Smoke Signals*, a film written, directed, and acted by Native Americans, then we discuss how these images present an alternative to traditional Hollywood stereotypes. If students can discern the components of racial stereotypes in a visual medium, they can transfer that skill to written forms.

An anticipatory activity to begin a unit on any Shakespearean play can explore the position of Shakespearean texts in contemporary popular culture. I have used the "To be or not to be" soliloquy from Zefferelli's version of *Hamlet* and the opening scene in the classroom from *The Last Action Hero*, featuring Arnold Schwarzenegger as action hero Jack Slater, declaiming the same famous soliloquy in a trailer that reimagines *Hamlet* as an action flick. In viewing the first clip, students examine how Zefferelli shoots the soliloquy using techniques of lighting and camera placement and the setting to clarify key points in the language of the speech. Looking at camera placement they easily recognize how the medium of film enhances the intimacy of the soliloquy through the use of the close-up. To link the examination of the clip to the position of a Shakespearean text in recent popular culture, they consider how the casting of Mel Gibson in the title role was, and still is, a controversial choice. As they move on to *The Last Action Hero* clip, they examine the use of the conventions of the movie trailer, the construction of the contemporary action hero persona, the use of color and black-and-white footage, and excerpts from Shakespeare's text to create a spoof. In the first chapter of their book, *Shakespeare: The Movie*, Lynda E. Boose and Richard Burt (1997) provide a helpful reading of *The Last Action Hero* sequence as well as commentary on the casting of Gibson as Hamlet. Instead of focusing on *Hamlet*, teachers can also use clips from Zefferelli's and Luhrman's versions of *Romeo and Juliet* to examine the culture influences on the latter version and the striking different style in sound and visuals in each work. Using clips again as a discussion starter will acclimate students to viewing short clips with a specific analytical focus. During the study of the specific play itself, I use excerpts from feature-length films to discuss highlights of the play as well as problematic scenes or speeches by examining the cinematic strategies that help draw the viewer's attention to key elements of the text and the characters.

Using Feature-Length Films

Each semester I use at least one feature-length film as one of the "core" or essential texts of the curriculum in an Advanced Placement literature course. To introduce the technique of multiple narrative perspectives, I use the film *Reversal of Fortune* to examine that technique in a cinematic form. A specific lesson plan for this film is featured in Chapter 6. I developed a course about ten years ago called Modern World Literature, in which teachers are required to screen at least two feature-length films to complement the study of two of the novels or plays used in the course. For example, after reading *All Quiet on the Western Front* students would screen and study *Gallipoli* to analyze how the relationships in the film mirror relationships in the novel as well as to examine how the brutality of war is visually depicted in both works. When reading Ibsen's *A Doll House*, students will view selected clips from a stage version on videotape to discuss choices that the actors and the director makes in bringing the play to life. After students have completed reading the play and viewing the performance excerpts, they view a companion film like *My Brilliant Career* in its entirety to analyze how characters, incidents, and themes are presented in another work that focuses on women's choices in marriage and career—in this instance in early twentieth-century Australia instead of nineteenth-century Norway. Chapter 6 features an appendix that matches a wide of range literary works with companion films commonly used in American, British, and world literature classes. Studying a film in its entirety requires a full week of classes to properly preview, view, and discuss the cinematic text in order to demonstrate to students that films have levels of richness akin to literature. I also routinely include a formal essay option that focuses on the analysis of a film viewed by the student outside of class in relation to a novel or play that has been read in class. Some of these options include the following:

Film Companion for *The Sound and the Fury*

- If you were intrigued by our analysis of *Reversal of Fortune*, you may compare the manipulation of point of view and chronology in another film, *Citizen Kane*. You should view the film more than once; but if that is impossible, then scan through the film a second time to re-view key scenes in order to discuss them with the same level of intensity that you would a scene from a written text.

- Carefully consider how the film manages to create a psychologically complex portrait of Charles Foster Kane as well as the people who tell their version of his story. Actually consider how many versions are told—not just four as one might think, considering their are four "narrators." Which accounts are more reliable? How do you know?

- Your essay should focus on the common characteristics that the film and novel share in terms of chronology, point of view, theme, and motifs (in film these are obviously visual, not verbal). The most important question to ask is if a visual text—such as a film—can develop narrative elements with the same complexity that a written text can. Make sure that you provide sufficient evidence.

Film Analysis Essay Option for *Richard III*

- Screen the most recent film adaptation of *Richard III*, starring Ian McKellen, Robert Downey, Jr., and Annette Bening. Examine the transfer of the story from medieval England to a twentieth-century context. Consider the changes or cuts made in the play and the decisions made in the design and costuming.

- Narrow your focus to the examination of one or two characters or two or three scenes. In discussing those characters and scenes, carefully describe and evaluate the choices made in visual and auditory techniques to bring the characters and situation to life on the screen.

- Pick up a copy of an article on the film adaptation from a text called *Shakespeare: The Movie* (available in the classroom). Supplement that reading with two reviews of the film (*Time* magazine ran an article the winter that the film debuted that discusses the spate of Shakespearean films that were released that year—both of these articles can be found on reputable Internet sites). Incorporate a discussion of how the film was received and reviewed in your analysis.

Film Analysis Essay Option for *The Turn of the Screw*

- There have been several film versions of the novel, but the most interesting is a British production made in the '60s called *The Innocents*. What is truly notable about it is the fact that the script was written by Truman Capote (author of *In Cold Blood*, among other works).
- Examine the extent to which the film is a faithful and successful adaptation of the novel. How does it handle the depiction of the governess and her perceptions of the children and the ghosts? To what extent is it able to depict the governess' psychological state? How does it manipulate the viewer's perception of the children? Is ultimately a novel like *The Turn of the Screw* "unfilmable"? What are the film's best moments? worst? Explain.
- You may choose to compare a key sequence from *The Innocents* with a more recent BBC adaptation of *The Turn of the Screw* adapted by Nick Dear and directed by Ben Bolt. Carefully describe and evaluate the use of cinematic techniques used in each version.

These writing options expand students' viewing repertoire and continue to legitimize the use of cinematic texts alongside traditional literary ones.

Students may initially balk at the critical focus placed on an activity that they perceive as pleasurable and as part of their leisure activities. By gradually acquainting them with these concepts, they will find them less burdensome. My students love to share how they are helping parents, siblings, and friends to better appreciate the media they are watching by explaining composition, editing, and sound techniques.

Films Cited

The Art of Film series, 1975, Perspective Films, NR, 20–25 min. per volume.

Avalon, 1991, Barry Levinson, PG, 126 min.

Basic Film Terms: A Visual Dictionary, 1970, Sheldon Renan, NR, 14 min.

Citizen Kane, 1941, Orson Welles, NR, 120 min.

Fantasia, 1940, Samuel Armstrong, et al., NR, 120 min.

Fantasia 2000, 2000, Hendel Butoy, et al., G, 74 min.

Gallipoli, 1981, Peter Weir, PG, 111 min.

The Great Train Robbery, 1902, Edwin S. Porter, NR, 12 min.

Jack Zipes
Disney

Hamlet, 1990, Franco Zefferelli, PG, 135 min.

The Innocents, 1961, Jack Clayton, NR, 99 min.

Jacob's Ladder, 1990, Adrian Lyne, R, 115 min.

The Last Action Hero, 1992, John McTiernan, PG, 120 min.

The Last of the Mohicans, 1992, Michael Mann, R, 122 min.

Meshes of the Afternoon, Maya Deren: Experimental Films, 1943–59, NR, 14 min.

The Movies Begin series, 1994, David Shepard, Kino Video, NR, 85–105 min. per volume.

My Brilliant Career, 1979, Gillian Armstrong, PG, 110 min.

My Man Godfrey, 1936, Gregory La Cava, NR, 93 min.

North by Northwest, 1959, Alfred Hitchcock, NR, 136 min.

Notorious, 1946, Alfred Hitchcock, NR, 101 min.

Peter Pan, 1953, Hamilton Luske, et al., NR, 76 min.

Potemkin (aka *The Battleship Potemkin*), 1925, Sergei Eisenstein, NR, 70 min.

Psycho, 1960, Alfred Hitchcock, NR, 109 min.

Reversal of Fortune, 1990, Barbet Schroeder, R, 120 min.

Richard III, 1995, Richard Loncraine, R, 104 min.

Romeo and Juliet, 1968, Franco Zefferelli, NR, 138 min.

Smoke Signals, 1997, Chris Eyre, PG-13, 89 min.

Stagecoach, 1939, John Ford, NR, 95 min.

The Thin Red Line, 1998, Terence Malick, R, 170 min.

A Trip to the Moon, 1903, Georges Melies, NR, 12 min.

True Stories: A Film About a Bunch of People in Virgil Texas, 1986, David Byrne, PG, 90 min.

The Turn of the Screw, 2000, Ben Bolt, NR, 120 min.

William Shakespeare's Romeo and Juliet, 1996, Baz Luhrman, R, 120 min.

Works Cited

BOOSE, LYNDA E., AND RICHARD BURT. 1997. *Shakespeare: The Movie*. New York: Routledge.

BORDWELL, DAVID, AND KRISTIN THOMPSON. 1986. *Film Art: An Introduction*. New York: Knopf.

FAULKNER, WILLIAM. 1929. *The Sound and the Fury*. Noel Polk, ed. New York: Vintage, 1990.

GENETTE, GERARD. 1980. *Narrative Discourse: An Essay in Method*. Ithaca, NY: Cornell University Press.

IBSEN, HENRICH. 1979. *A Doll House. Ibsen: Four Major Plays*. Vol. 1. Rolf Fjelde, trans. New York: Signet Classic, 1965.

JAMES, HENRY. 1898. *The Turn of the Screw and Other Short Novels*. New York: Signet, 1995.

MAST, GERALD, AND BRUCE F. KAWIN. 2000. *A Short History of Film*. 7th ed. Boston, MA: Allyn and Bacon.

REMARQUE, ERICH MARIA. 1929. *All Quiet on the Western Front*. A. W. Green, trans. New York: Fawcett Crest, 1987.

SOBCHACK, THOMAS, AND VIVIAN SOBCHACK. 1987. *An Introduction to Film*. Glenview, IL: Scott Foresman.

TRUFFAUT, FRANCOIS. 1983. *Hitchcock/Truffaut*. Rev. ed. New York: Simon and Schuster.

WELCH, JAMES. 1986. *Fools Crow*. New York: Penguin.

FIVE

Analyzing the Moving Image: Strategies

MARY T. CHRISTEL

Once students have acquired a set of terms to describe the moving image, the task becomes how to apply and master the use of those terms in a variety of short, highly focused activities before moving on to a feature-length film or television episode. This chapter begins with "hands-on" activities, since a major component of visual and media literacy is to have students produce media texts. The analysis of other texts becomes more meaningful once students have made similar decisions in composition, editing, and sound elements. These activities can be both high or low tech based on the resources of a particular classroom or the expertise of the teacher.

Designing Storyboards with Students

The easiest and most fundamental way to get students to pay attention to the many elements that compose a single sequence is to have students actually design a sequence. To begin, give students copies of storyboard forms. Notice that the story-board form in Figure 5–1 is a refinement of the storyboard form used for the twelve-shot activity in Chapter 1. The drawings on a storyboard need only be stick figures and crude elements of scenery and props, but it is critical to have students describe the content of each shot—explaining placement, arrangement, lighting, important elements of color, and framing (as it applies). The sound element column should include details related to dialogue, sound effects, music, and key background sound. Finally, an editing technique needs to be identified between the drawing of each shot. An effective first storyboarding activity involves giving all students a basic situation to storyboard, like a child sneaking out of the house, a policeman chasing a fleeing mugger, or kids looking for a lost pet. Once storyboards are completed, students can compare their treatment of a single, simple sequence. Students can also experiment with literary adaptation by storyboarding small sections of a short story, play, or novel. This is a particularly effective warm-up activity prior to screening and analyzing a film adaptation of a story or book studied by the entire class. This technique helps students

Sketch of shot

Provide a written
description of shot
visual and sound
elements below:

Editing Transition:

Editing Transition:

Editing Transition:

Figure 5–1. *Storyboard Form*

understand that words create very powerful images, and the recognition of this concept can stimulate more careful and critical reading habits in those students.

If students have completed the twelve-shot activity described in Chapter 1, a logical extension of that storyboarding activity would be to actually shoot the sequence as a live-action narrative. This version of the sequence should be no more than two minutes in length.

Designing a Soundscape

The previous chapter highlighted the most traditional way to analyze the impact of sound by turning down the volume on a scene rich in and dependent on sound to examine the impact of the sound added to the second viewing of that sequence. An even better way to sensitize students to the importance of sound in creating a narrative and setting the mood would be to create a story based solely on sound. Now this assignment may seem antithetical to a chapter titled "Analyzing the Moving Image," but contemporary filmgoers sometimes take sound for granted. We cannot fully appreciate sound until it is separated and isolated from the visual image.

SOUNDSCAPE ACTIVITY

I call this assignment a "soundscape." The first time I participated in an activity similar to this, I was in a class focusing on group dynamics in classroom settings. Groups of three students went out into the school building to collect and create sounds in order to tell a story. We had to record the sounds in sequence and have a finished product ready in about forty-five minutes. The emphasis there was on working together as group rather than the aesthetic qualities of our work. Here is my adaptation of that assignment, with a greater emphasis on production values and aesthetic results.

Students design and record a one-minute audiotape that tells a story purely through music, sound effects, background sound, and only five words (the words are optional). They may create the sound effects through their own efforts or take them from sound effects recordings.

Students should keep the situation simple to concentrate on creating a mood, and devise a simple series of actions articulated through sound to develop that mood. Sinister or creepy scenarios tend to work best, but students certainly are limited only by their imaginations. An effective "sinister scenario" could describe someone trying to break into a house. The soundscape artist would need to create sound effects of the intruder walking, breaking glass or prying a window open, crawling through that window, opening drawers, rummaging through the homeowner's belongings, and finally being caught. A scenario that doesn't focus on criminal behavior could record a person's morning routine: alarm sounding, music playing, washing a face, brushing teeth, dressing, and eating breakfast while reading the morning paper. To put a twist on this situation, that person could discover it is Saturday by looking at the date on the paper, and the only words uttered in the piece could draw the audience's attention to that fact.

Their planning activities begin with writing a paragraph scenario that describes the situation, and includes setting, characters, and actions. Sean planned his soundscape by developing this scenario:

> There is a terrible storm on the night of the last football game of the season, and the quarterback is preparing the team for the final play of their high school careers. He preps them and there is the crowd yelling in the background as the quarterback and the team take the line. There is the snap and the quarterback scans the field for the correct person to throw the ball to. He finally picks the one man that hasn't caught a pass all season—me. I catch the ball and run it back for a touchdown without realizing that I have been tackled in the end zone and am badly injured. This shows my love for the team and desire to win. They do, and the crowd, in the middle of the storm, goes nuts.

After developing a scenario, the student must create a cue sheet that lists in proper order each sound and its duration (number of seconds) that will be laid down on the tape. The cue sheet could also cite the source of the sound (CD, tape, live creation). Here is how Sean prepared his cue sheet:

Cue Sheet

Action	*Time in Sequence*
Begin playing Pachelbel's "Canon in D"	0–60 seconds
Begin storm noises	off and on for 5–60 seconds
"Guys this is it . . . Break"	starting at 10, ending at 15 seconds
On the line, "Set . . . Hut"	starting at 20, ending at 30
Pumping with the ball with hand	starting 30, ending 33
Grunt No. 1 with throwing ball	starting 34, ending 36
Whistling ball	starting 36, ending 40
Sound of ball hitting hands	starting 40, ending 42
Sound of feet on the ground	starting 42, ending 55
"I can see it"	starting 43, ending 45
Grunt No. 2 with running and avoiding tackles	starting 43, ending 55

Heartbeat	starting 42, ending 55
"Oh Yes"	starting 50, ending 51
Cheering	starting 51, ending 55
Ambulance siren	starting 55, ending 57
"Oh No"	starting 58, ending 60

After students have completed the project, they should write a one-page reflection on the process and compare it to the planning, execution, and success of their twelve-shot activity (see Chapter 1) if that activity has been part of their preparation. Sean evaluates his process in this manner:

> The audiotape that corresponds to this project was much more difficult than the twelve-shot sequence, because of differences in planning and execution, as well as the overall resulting product of the audiotape. Personally, I found this project really challenging, but with the help of some other sound makers (my stepfather and our piano), I felt pretty confident of my accomplishment in this project. I think that it turned out pretty well.

> The one-minute audio recording was a lot more difficult to plan than was the twelve-shot sequence, because it was hard to hear exactly what was to be recorded by the tape. By this I mean that unlike in the visual project where the design of a storyboard was completely necessary, the development of the cue sheet was a lot harder to follow. I thought my cue sheet was pretty in depth, but as I reflect, I realize that my timing was way off on some of the sounds, and I actually used more words than was allowed. This was my best take, however, so I had to leave them in, and anyway, they were just a few "Oh yes"s. The storyboard for the visual picture activity was really helpful in planning the shots out, but the cue sheet, I thought, really didn't help too much to make the recording accurate.

> The execution was also really different, because it was a lot easier to set up a "shot," but it is really hard to get the mood right in the audio presentation. For example, in one take, my cat ran in between my legs and I accidentally stepped on him causing a loud "Meow" on the final recording. This was not planned, and I, as a result, was required to get rid of that take. The final result of this project, after spending close to a few days on it was really disappointing, but as I listened to it, I realized that I didn't do as bad as I had thought. Even though my picture sequence came out much better, I feel that, after working my behind off, this project taught me a lot on the usage of sound and preparing me to use sound in my own films.

Notice that Sean anticipates the connection between this activity and the video that he will shoot later in the semester.

An extension to the soundscape assignment could involve distributing the finished soundscapes to members of the class so that no student has his or her own. Students then create a storyboard to illustrate the narrative sequence of sound. The storyboard eventually would be given back to the soundscape creator for his or her reaction. For classes that have access to the proper equipment and time to shoot and edit the footage, those storyboards could become live-action sequences, staying within the one-minute time limit of the original soundscape. Actually, the more the teacher limits the duration of students' early shooting activities, the more fruitful the results. Novice film-makers tend to linger too long on a single shot or sequence as a whole.

Using Film Extracts

Using short scenes for the application of composition, editing, and sound terminology is best. Students need the opportunity to watch a single sequence several times in order to fully identify and analyze the many techniques at work. Teachers can certainly select sequences to screen and discuss, but there is a useful series of film extracts distributed on video by Coronet Films, called *The Art of Film*. It is a twelve-volume set, with useful volumes focusing on camerawork, editing, and sound. Each volume of film extracts also includes a voice-over narrator, Rod Serling or Douglas Fairbanks, Jr., who helps students identify the techniques at work in each sequence. When I screen these excerpts, I furnish students with a series of questions to help them take appropriate notes. Here is an example of the kinds of questions that I pose for volume 2, "The Camera" (20 minutes long). I ask students to answer the following questions after they view the excerpts.

Beauty and the Beast by Jean Cocteau (1:02–4:40)
- Where did Cocteau get his inspiration for the visual style of the film?
- Describe how lighting sets the mood.
- How is matchcut editing used to create an illusion?

Two English Girls by Francois Truffaut (4:42–6:15)
- How does Truffaut maintain the intimacy of the scene?
- What type of shot is used throughout this scene? Why is it used?

The Rocking Horse Winner by Desmond Dickson (6:16–8:04)
- How is point of view or subjective camerawork used?
- Why is it used?

The Lady Vanishes by Alfred Hitchcock (8:05–10:22)
- What is Hitchcock's theory of creating suspense?
- How does the camera control the wine glasses? Give two examples of shots used.
- Give an example of a rack focus shot.

The Most Dangerous Game by David O. Selznick (10:24–13:32)

- How is the viewer thrust into the chase?
- How does this clip use stock footage?

The Silence by Ingmar Bergman (13:34–16:04)

- How is the boy's isolation emphasized visually?
- How does the camera replace dialogue in the last sequence in the bedroom?

Shadows of Forgotten Ancestors by Parazanov (16:05–end)

- How is the illusion of the tree falling on the woodcutter achieved?

Teachers should feel free to use extracts from films like these as warm-up activities for watching particular kinds of film. In a given class, it might not be practical or necessary to screen all the extracts in a particular volume. It might be most useful to select the sequences that feature key techniques that are prominently used in a film that will soon be screened in its entirety in class.

If a teacher does not have access to *The Art of Film* series, it is easy enough to select extracts from well-known films to use to illustrate particular visual and sound strategies. For example, two sequences from John Ford's *Stagecoach* (1939)—the Apache raid sequence, and the shootout that ends the film—provide engaging and basic material that can be discussed in terms of visual composition and sound. Lighting and motifs in the shootout scene are also worth discussing. It is very important not to overwhelm students with too many questions. It is most effective to have students screen a sequence the first time without asking any questions and focus the initial phase of the discussion on what they notice on that first viewing. Note the increase in the number of questions for the second scene. Each scene could and should be a day's lesson. It is important to show the sequence more than once, each time with increasing sophistication of viewing focus. It also is important to periodically talk through a sequence after students have seen it more than once by using the pause feature on the remote to isolate key shots.

The Apache Raid

- In the opening of the scene, what makes the stagecoach look vulnerable? Cite two shots (and describe the arrangement and placement of each).
- When is sound a critical factor in communicating what we cannot see? Cite two examples.
- Find examples of all of the following techniques used to heighten the suspense or drama of the attack:

  framing

  arrangement

  placement

  tracking

  panning

The Shootout

- What makes the overall setting a little unusual for a climactic shootout scene?
- What string of visual and verbal motifs foreshadow Luke Plummer's death?
- What kinds of sounds (including silence) heighten the suspense?
- At what times is the viewer able to rely only on sound to know what is happening?
- How is humor used to break the tension of the sequence? Cite examples that are visual and verbal.
- How is subjective camerawork used effectively right after the shootout is over?

Editing

The next important aspect of film technique is editing. It is the aspect that some students find difficult to grasp, so it is important initially to examine rather extreme examples. A film filled with innovative editing techniques is *Citizen Kane*. Two sequences that are most useful and very short are the breakfast sequence and Susan Alexander's opera tour. The breakfast sequence is located at the beginning of Leland's section. Leland is trying to explain the disintegration of Kane's marriage to his first wife, Emily Monroe Norton. Sixteen years of marriage is condensed into a two-minute sequence that shows them at the breakfast table. Each shot reflects a different stage in their marriage. Students should focus on how dialogue, costuming, props, and the table itself communicate the state of their marriage. At the beginning of the sequence they are sitting next to each other at a relatively small dining table making playful small talk about the parties they've attended and the time of day, with Emily fetchingly dressed in evening wear. By the end of the sequence Emily looks almost puritanical as she reads the newspaper of Kane's competitor and speaks not a word (and neither does Kane) while the camera moves back to reveal a table that has grown longer over the years and that now separates each of them as they sit at opposite ends. During Susan Alexander's prolonged section toward the end of the film, she covers a grueling opera tour that spans many cities by superimposing and dissolving the front pages of newspapers with images of Susan on stage and a pulsing stage light in close-up. Sound is critical in this sequence. Susan's hideous singing is layered with the sound of some machine winding down. The sequence ends and there is a cut to a provocative image of a glass, spoon, and medicine bottle on a tray in sharp close-up in the foreground; someone (Susan) breathing in a labored fashion in a bed obscured by shadow in the middle ground; and an illuminated door in the background. Combining this with the opera tour sequence, the viewer deduces that Susan has tried to commit suicide, using whatever is in the bottle in the foreground, as a result of her experiences on the tour. Teachers planning to use sequences from *Citizen Kane* should consult

Robert Carringer's (1985) meticulous study of the film, *The Making of Citizen Kane*, for further information regarding the innovative techniques used in the film.

A more challenging and sophisticated application of editing can be found in "The Odessa Steps" section of Sergei Eisenstein's silent film *Potemkin*. This particular sequence depicts civilians, who have come to the aid of sailors on the *Battleship Potemkin*, hunted down by Tsarists soldiers. In this sequence, Eisenstein expands the time it would take for the soldiers to march down the steps and massacre the assembled civilians. He tells the stories of several civilians who are trapped on the steps and shot or maimed by the soldiers. One of the signature images is a baby carriage that careens down the steps after the baby's mother is shot in the abdomen. It is very important to have students view the sequence without much preparatory information to see what they can understand of the narrative purely through the images presented and the few title cards that appear on the screen. Students can use the following list for discussion or written response after the first viewing of "The Odessa Steps":

- Briefly summarize the sequence of events that the sequence develops.
- How easy or difficult was it to follow this sequence of events?
- How would you describe the method of editing that was used to put these shots together?
- How many verbal messages accompanied the action?
- Cite four single images that were the most memorable, shocking, or intriguing. Describe them in very specific detail.

After the students discuss their impressions of the narrative, they should note which images are particularly vivid and memorable and what makes each of these images so. A second viewing should focus on more critical analysis of the techniques of montage that are employed. The particular way a director edits cuts to control the film's meaning and effect is called *montage* (Mast and Kawin 2000, 165–167).

Lev Kuleshov, a Russian film teacher, divided cuts into three categories:

A *narrative cut* develops story through the use of straight cuts, flashback, cross-cut, or associative cut (revealing thoughts).

An *intellectual cut* links ideas represented by objects or people through the use of a visual metaphor (linking two visual images in successive shots).

An *emotional cut* reveals the emotion of the character on screen or provokes an emotional response in the viewer through a combination of two or more shots.

A cut could work on all three levels. Teachers should prepare to discuss this sequence by reading Gerald Mast and Bruce Kawin's analysis in *A Short History of the Movies*, which is well illustrated with shots from "The Odessa Steps" sequence. The following suggestions are helpful guides after the second viewing of "The Odessa Steps."

- Cite one example for each of the following cuts as they are found in the excerpt that you view:

  a narrative cut

  an intellectual cut

  an emotional cut

- "Eisenstein defined his principle of montage as one of collision, of conflict, of contrast"(Mast and Kawin 2000, 168). Select three moments from "The Odessa Steps" sequence that visually best reflect collision, conflict, or contrast. It would be best to describe a combination of two shots for each example. For example, the combination of two shots—one showing a mother climbing up the steps with a wounded child in her arms; the second showing the line of soldiers who shot the boys climbing down the stairs, closing the gap between them. The first shot emphasizes the agony of the mother; the second shot does not reveal the expressions of the soldiers, in contrast to the mother, so they appear to be automatons.

- Eisenstein recognized the power of symbol and metaphor. In earlier sections of the film a plate inscribed with "Give us our daily bread" is smashed by a disgruntled sailor to reflect the growing unrest of the crew (170). A crucifix is raised in a threatening manner by a priest confronting a crew member; then there is a cut to an officer raising his sword to a crew member. What might each of the following represent or parallel in "The Odessa Steps"?

  the runaway baby carriage

  the three lions

- As earlier noted, Eisenstein's focus is on the mass of humanity, yet he recognized how that mass is made up of individuals. Explain how this is evident in the fourth part of the film, "The Odessa Steps." Eisenstein expands, or stretches, the time of "The Odessa Steps" sequence through his montage. How does he achieve this expansion of time? What techniques does he use? What might his purpose be in using this technique for this sequence?

The analysis of this famous sequence can be extended with a screening of a scene from Brian DePalma's *The Untouchables*. The scene places Eliot Ness and his partner, Stone, at Union Station waiting to apprehend Al Capone's bookkeeper. A shootout ensues on the marble steps of the train station and a woman and her baby in a carriage get caught in the crossfire. DePalma discusses his inspiration for this sequence in an article in the first edition of *Premiere* magazine. Similarly, Arthur Penn expands time through montage techniques in the final scene of *Bonnie and Clyde*, where the two bank robbers are ambushed and brutally shot to death. Linking "The Odessa Steps" with contemporary films helps students recognize the influence of classic filmmakers on contemporary directors.

Point of View

It is hard to avoid discussing Hitchcock when it comes to examining the use of the camera to achieve a compelling point-of-view shot. His film *Notorious* is filled with examples of subjective and authorial shots. The film opens with a group of reporters waiting outside a Miami courtroom. One of the shots in that sequence visually implies that the viewer is someone, ostensibly one of those reporters, peering through a crack in the courtroom door to hear the final words of a man being tried for treason. Later in the film, the leading female character, Alicia Huberman, wakes in her bed suffering from a tremendous hangover. The camera adopts her view as she watches U.S. agent, T. R. Devlin, walk into her room. The camera brings Devlin into focus and rotates to show him at an unusual overhead angle to mimic Alicia's view from a prone position in the bed. The most complex use of point of view is in the scene very late in the film when the audience begins to suspect that Alicia is being drugged or poisoned by something in her coffee. In several scenes coffee cups are in the presented foreground and in close-up in a highly authorial manner. Visual emphasis of the coffee cups certainly makes them one of Hitchcock's *plastics*, objects that heighten suspense or move the plot. Examining the manipulation of point of view helps students to recognize that elements of literature are also present in film texts. Extracts from *Psycho*, *Rear Window*, and *Suspicion* also provide excellent models to discuss the manipulation of point of view.

Using Avant-Garde Short Films

Short films present a complete narrative supported by the visual and auditory choices made by a director, so students can analyze a complete cinematic text from start to finish in a single class period. The best source of short pieces comes from the avant-garde films of Maya Deren. She created a series of surreal films in the '40s and '50s, including her most famous work, "Meshes of the Afternoon." She utilizes a variety of techniques to create a fourteen-minute film that challenges the viewer's notion of what is real and what is imagined. The central female character glimpses a passing figure on a road who leaves a flower in her path. The film then creates a series of events and images that oddly evolve from that single opening event. The viewer is left to wonder if the subsequent events are merely in the mind of the central character. In their analysis of the film, Wead and Lellis note that Deren develops a basic sequence of action that is repeated three times throughout the film to create a narrative structure, but that narrative structure is never meant to be realistic and actually resists a definitive interpretation (1981, 411). This kind of cinematic text becomes a rich source for discussion of directors' choices and the critical, interpretive judgments that viewers are required to make to come to a personal understanding of the text. Here are a range of questions to give students a viewing focus. The film could be the tool to examine only one aspect or the complete range of its cinematic techniques.

- What is the basic pattern of action that is repeated three times? What are the critical variations in the second and third versions?
- What are important objects in the narrative? How do the camera and sound effects draw the viewer's attention to them? Which of these objects are *leitmotifs*? What do these objects add to the meaning of the narrative?
- To what extent is sound synchronized with action?
- What are repeated sound motifs? With what types of images are these motifs coordinated?
- At what points in the narrative does the director rely primarily on subjective or authorial shots? What kind of images does she present through neutral camerawork?
- When does the director make effective use of extreme camera angles?
- Why is stop motion photography used?
- What is the most compelling image in the film? What makes it so?

Obviously, a film like this lends itself to several viewings. This film also lends itself to writing activities that encourage students to develop an interpretation of the narrative based on the cinematic techniques employed by the director. The students could narrate the "story" of one of the characters presented by Deren. What brings the character to this environment, what is his or her desire or object, and what is the character's impression of what happens once he or she enters that environment? Students could also examine which cinematic elements provide the most powerful clues in determining a reasonable interpretation of the piece. More sophisticated students then could move on to designing storyboards for their own avant-garde sequence and writing an explanatory scenario to accompany the storyboard.

Teachers should never be afraid to introduce a challenging or unfamiliar film text in order to help students analyze its visual and auditory properties. Encountering these texts in short or excerpted forms introduces students to films outside of the mainstream or their immediate viewing experience and hopefully helps them develop a greater awareness of the diversity of film art.

Films Cited

The Art of Film series, 1975, Perspective Films, NR, 20–25 min. per volume.

Bonnie and Clyde, 1967, Arthur Penn, NR, 112 min.

Citizen Kane, 1941, Orson Welles, NR, 120 min.

"Meshes of the Afternoon," *Maya Deren: Experimental Films*, 1943–59, NR, 14 min.

North by Northwest, 1959, Alfred Hitchcock, NR, 136 min.

Notorious, 1946, Alfred Hitchcock, NR, 101 min.

Potemkin (aka *The Battleship Potemkin*), 1925, Sergei Eisenstein, NR, 70 min.

Psycho, 1960, Alfred Hitchcock, NR, 109 min.

Rear Window, 1954, Alfred Hitchcock, NR, 112 min.

Stagecoach, 1939, John Ford, NR, 95 min.

Suspicion, 1941, Alfred Hitchcock, NR, 102 min.

The Untouchables, 1987, Brian DePalma, R, 119 min.

Works Cited

CARRINGER, ROBERT. 1985. *The Making of Citizen Kane*. Berkeley, CA: University of California Press.

KORNBLUTH, JESSE. 1987. "The Untouchables: Shot by Shot." *Premiere* (July/August): 36–40.

MAST, GERALD, AND BRUCE F. KAWIN. 2000. *A Short History of Film*. 7th ed. Boston, MA: Allyn and Bacon.

WEAD, GEORGE, AND GEORGE LELLIS. 1981. *Film: Form and Function*. Boston, MA: Houghton Mifflin.

SIX

Film in the Literature Class: Not Just Dessert Anymore

MARY T. CHRISTEL

The use of film in a typical literature class has been seriously questioned or even vilified for many years, because film is commonly integrated, if you could call it that, at the end of the study of a novel or play as a "reward." Students commonly need only to stay awake through the several days' screening of a feature-length adaptation and perhaps engage in a cursory analysis of what the filmmaker added to or subtracted from the original literary source material. Film is just the dessert after a multicourse repast of reading, writing, and testing.

Film can be so much more than just a reward or a time to relax for patient and reluctant readers of a text. It can provide meaningful enrichment, even for the eager reader, who can access visual texts with very sophisticated insights cultivated by the careful reading and understanding of a literary text. With the availability of many feature-length adaptations and animated versions of literature as well as documentaries and informational videos, teachers can integrate a variety of texts and techniques to enhance the study of most literary texts. This chapter is designed to offer a range of instructional strategies that are modeled here for one text or literary technique, but these strategies can easily be adapted to many titles and for many student abilities.

Providing Motivation for Reading

Perhaps the most daunting task facing a literature teacher is mustering the fortitude to embark on the study of a Shakespeare play with reluctant readers. For such students, film can generate the motivation needed by providing a stimulating introduction to Shakespeare's career and to a particular play. Helping students understand the context of the writer's career can foster an interest in the text itself. The Arts and Entertainment channel's *Biography* series has produced entertaining and informative installments on writers from the high school canon, including Shakespeare. The episode on Shakespeare combines visuals with the standard voice-over narration to help students come to understand not only Shakespeare the man and the writer but also the cultural and political environment that produced his works. If the fifty-minute format of the *Biography* segment, "William Shakespeare: Life in Drama," is too long for a single class period, the *Famous Authors* series offers a thirty-minute program focusing on much the same material in a more condensed form. As part of its educational outreach surrounding the release of *Shakespeare in Love*, Miramax produced and distributed *Shakespeare in the Classroom*, a forty-five-minute film that features narration by the stars of the feature-length film along with clips that illustrate Shakespeare's life and times. This program is especially useful when introducing *Romeo and Juliet*.

If helping students become familiar with the plot of a particular play rather than its historical context is of paramount importance, teachers should take advantage of *Shakespeare: The Animated Tales*. These thirty-minute adaptations of *Romeo and Juliet*, *Macbeth*, *Hamlet*, *The Tempest*, *A Midsummer Night's Dream*, and *Twelfth Night* were originally aired on HBO and produced by a British-Russian team of actors and animators. I have used these films as a means to preview the essential parts of the plot. Since these short films abbreviate the plot and eliminate some characters or scenes, there is still much for students to discover in the nuances of character, plot, and theme as they read the text.

If a teacher does not have access to these tapes, she can make her own tape that highlights key scenes from a filmed version of a specific play. Goldhill Video has developed a series of tapes called *Understanding Shakespeare: The Tragedies* that select key scenes from *Macbeth*, *Hamlet*, *Othello*, and *Romeo and Juliet*. Each tape runs ninety minutes and provides scenes that trace the bare bones of plot and characterization with a cue sheet that makes finding each scene very easy. Each scene is also accompanied by a commentary by a panel of scholars. Their comments are very accessible for even the most reluctant reader of Shakespeare. This is a perfect tool for a teacher who is able to keep a video recorder and monitor in his room for the duration of a unit on a Shakespeare play. As students are stumped, the teacher can choose to show the scene alone for close analysis or show the scene with the related commentary.

A real curiosity in short-format adaptations of Shakespearean plays can be found in a collection titled *Silent Shakespeare*. It features silent film versions of *The Tempest*, *A Midsummer Night's Dream*, *King Lear*, *Twelfth Night*, *The Merchant of Venice*, and *Richard III* dating from 1899–1911. Screening these adaptations could lead students to create their own condensed versions of a play and to put the performance on videotape, either in a silent or sound version.

As students read a given play such as *Romeo and Juliet*, consider showing a feature-length version of the play act by act. Watching the acts in this fashion helps students who are more visually attuned in their learning style to better understand the text and provides another take on the text for students who are struggling with the reading of the text. Treating the viewing of the film in this manner can also afford the teacher the opportunity to discuss choices that the director makes in adapting the play to the screen for modern audiences as well as the director's use of images to illustrate and augment the language of the text.

Using a documentary film to take students behind the scenes of an actual production of a Shakespeare play prior to reading the text can prove to be the best motivational tool. In preparation for reading *Hamlet*, try screening *Discovering Hamlet*, which follows the rehearsal process of a youthful Kenneth Branagh being directed by veteran actor Derek Jacobi. The sixty-minute documentary focuses on the essential scenes and characters of the play, so it prepares students to better understand the plot, to gain insight into the characters' motivations for action and nonaction, and to witness the challenges these roles present modern-day actors and directors. A film like this could be shown just in excerpt form. A teacher might show a portion of a film prior to reading the text and continue screening the rest of the film incrementally throughout the course of reading the play. I have used Al Pacino's *Looking for Richard* as an introduction to *Richard III* with my AP students. Generally, I wouldn't assume that advanced-level students need the priming of plot and character that a film of this sort provides, but Pacino goes on to explore the need to perform Shakespeare for modern audiences, the popularity of *Richard III*, and the problems of mounting a history play for audiences little schooled in English history. This viewing activity provides a rich resource for discussing the play throughout the reading process. The only complaint that my students lodge is that they cannot get the image of Al Pacino as Richard III out of their heads as they read the text.

These prereading uses of film are certainly not limited to the study of Shakespeare. A teacher can show the A&E *Biography* episode on Charles Dickens prior to reading *Great Expectations*. A highlight tape could be crafted to preview the major incident of a nineteenth-century novel like *Jane Eyre*. Students could begin a study of Mary Shelley's *Frankenstein* by screening "The True Story of Frankenstein" from A&E. This program features segments on the development of the novel and its adaptation into more than one hundred film versions. For books like *The Scarlet Letter* or *Huckleberry Finn* teachers can use an episode from The Discovery Channel's *Great Books* series.

Exploring Literary Adaptation

A Way In: Character Dossier Activity

Early in my teaching experience, I was faced with sustaining a standard-level freshman class' interest in Dickens' *Great Expectations*. I wanted to build a personal commitment in each student, to help them read with interest and to engage their critical thinking skills through the end of the novel. Our department had just been equipped with a VCR and TV monitor on a cart that could be whisked into any classroom and a video cassette of *Great Expectations* (and one or two other videotapes that comprised our film library at that time). In order to invest the students in the text and, mindful of the "dessert" theory of film use, to have something meaningful to do with the viewing of the film, I assigned each student in the class a character in the novel. First, each student was required to create a dossier for his character based on textual support and

Very good Activity

to include several written journal entries based on the events presented in the three stages of the novel (someone like Mrs. Joe would write from her perch in the afterlife upon her demise to comment on events that occur after her death in the novel). The character dossier included the following questions:

- What are the most striking aspect of the character's physical appearance?
- What are his/her most distinguishing habits or mannerisms?
- What is this character's most prized possession? Explain how your choice is based on textual evidence or inference.
- How does this character become a part of Pip's life?
- To what extent is this character presented as a mysterious figure or a person who is harboring a secret?
- To what extent does this character seem to support or thwart Pip's "Great Expectations"?
- What does this character say directly about Pip?
- What does Pip say about this character? To what extent does Pip's opinion of this character change as his fortunes improve?
- To what extent is this character static or dynamic over the course of his/her appearance in the novel?

When it came time to screen the film, each student needed to take notes regarding the following:

- How does the actor playing the role match the description in the novel?
- How does the actor capture the specific habits and mannerisms you used to define the character as you read the novel?
- To what extent is the character's role expanded, reduced, or totally eliminated in the film? What seem to be the reasons why these changes were made in your character?

By the time we screened the film at the end of reading the novel, students felt a clear and meaningful connection with the treatment of their characters. As I recall, a few students were outraged at the diminishment of their beloved characters at the hands of a director, screenwriter, or editor. This experience provided a lively discussion about how difficult it is to compress a lengthy Victorian novel into a two-hour film format. Teachers can now use the several miniseries versions that have been produced by the BBC and the Disney Channel to compare the treatment of key characters.

Frankenstein: *Media Adaptation*

Television abounds with parodies of literature and episodes that are clearly informed by literary sources. An example is an episode from *The X-Files*, called "A Modern

Prometheus," which I have used in conjunction with the study of Mary Shelley's *Frankenstein*. Here are the questions that students use as they screen the episode in class:

- What are the basic conventions of an *X-Files* episode in terms of plot and characterization of Mulder and Scully?
- Which elements of the story or production design remind you of *Edward Scissorhands*? (This film was screened in class as part of a previous unit on satire.)
- What is the difference between a satire and a parody?

  How is it clear that this episode is a parody of the series?

  How does the episode satirize specific targets like small town life/attitudes and the media?
- Which elements of the *Frankenstein* story (derived from Mary Shelley or film sources) are used to develop the plot and give the episode its usual paranormal spin?

  Which elements are treated in a comic manner? Why?

  Which elements are treated more seriously?

  Which elements of the story are a perfect fit for an *X-Files* episode?
- When does the dialogue directly refer to the *Frankenstein* story?
- How does the presence of Cher (through music and film) add to the serious and surrealistic quality of the episode?
- Why do you think the producers of the series decided to create an episode that in a sense pokes fun at itself?

An episode like this one helps students explore the notion of *intertextuality*, the concept that one media text can comment on how it is connected to or borrows from other specific literary and pop culture texts. Obviously examining this episode involves a far more layered kind of adaptation than do the activities related to *Great Expectations*, but this more sophisticated approach is certainly suited to senior-level students, while the character study approach is a more comfortable fit with freshmen.

Narrative Structure

As more contemporary literature finds its ways into the high school literary canon, teachers need to prepare their students for unusual and problematic narrative structures. For students who are accustomed to reading highly linear plots with heavy doses of closure, narratives that are more loosely constructed and lacking in traditional elements of closure may prove difficult and unsatisfying. Hollywood films clearly train today's students to expect highly linear plots with direct connections between cause and effect. The best way to narratively retrain students' expectations is to study foreign films.

In preparation for a very episodic text like Sandra Cisneros' *House on Mango Street*, Francois Truffaut's films of childhood would provide interesting cultural companions. Obviously, his most famous film of this sort is his first, *The 400 Blows*. That film follows its protagonist, Antoine Doinel, as he becomes increasingly alienated from his parents, his school, and his only friend. The structure of the film's plot is clearly linear with strong patterns of cause and effect, but its pacing is decidedly slower than the conventional Hollywood treatment of an alienated child's exploits. Shooting in what is known as French New Wave style, the film does not have the high production values of a film American students would typically see and there is a decidedly improvisational quality about many of the scenes, but it is precisely this lack of Hollywood polish that gives the film its sense of realism. A later Truffaut film, *Small Change*, is lighter in tone and more decidedly episodic in nature. It follows the lives of about a dozen children, ranging in age from toddler to adolescent, in the town of Thiers. By weaving the exploits of these children from various backgrounds, Truffaut artfully pays homage to the unexpected strength and resilience of children. Some questions and suggestions to help focus student viewing follow.

Small Change (1974)

Director: Francois Truffaut
Screenplay: Francois Truffaut, Suzanne Schiffman

- Summarize the content of the film.
- As you watch the film, jot down details (other than language) that clearly mark it as a film that has not been made in the Hollywood studio system.
- Describe each of the following characters and identify the quality or aspect of childhood each represents. It helps to also identify the color or type of clothing each one wears to separate the characters.

  Patrick
  Leclou
  Gregory
  Laurent
  Richard Golfier
  DeLuca brothers
  Bruno
  Sylvie
  Corrine and Patricia

- How does Martine open and close the film?
- Give three examples of how the film presents typical children's behavior.
- Which aspects of the film are "French"? How are small-town life and childhood presented as culturally distinct from American customs and values?

[handwritten margin note: Reference this in my group]

73

- While the film views the world through the perspective of the children, it does present the view of the adults. Give three examples of this perspective.
- To what extent does the film present a central conflict?
- How are the vignettes (short scenes) unified? Which scenes or characters help to link episodes/events?
- What theme related to childhood is developed throughout the film? Give two examples to support your choice.
- Why is so much time devoted to Oscar in the newsreel? How does this relate to the theme?
- How do the following characteristics of French New Wave films contribute to the realism of the film?

> handheld camera
> natural lighting
> location shooting
> improvised plot and dialogue
> use of "nonactors"
> direct sound recording

After viewing a film like *Small Change*, which does not present a conventional narrative structure, students will be better prepared to read and understand written texts that follow the same loose narrative line. Similarly, film can prepare students to access stories that present complex shifting points of view and perspectives like Faulkner's *The Sound and the Fury* or N. Scott Momaday's *House Made of Dawn*.

I prepare my AP literature students for the study of *The Sound and the Fury* with the screening of *Reversal of Fortune*, the film adaptation of Alan Dershowitz's account of his involvement in the Claus von Bülow case. What drew me to this film in relation to Faulkner's four-perspective account of the Compson family is the presence of shifting perspectives in the film. Throughout the film, comatose Sunny von Bülow speaks directly to the viewer and narrates her version of the events leading up to her second and permanent coma, Claus presents his case to Dershowitz and his assistants, while Dershowitz pieces together the testimony of Sunny's maid and the deposition of a very shady David Marriot. I carefully plan what students will know by the end of each installment of the film to force them to determine which point of view they are willing to accept at that point in the viewing process. This strategy forces them to "read" the film recursively. Because of the way the differing stories are sequenced, viewers are continually forced to revise their perceptions of Sunny, Claus, and Dershowitz. Here is the manner in which I have broken the film down to fit into three fifty-minute class periods.

Reversal of Fortune

Direction: Barbet Schroeder
Screenplay: Nicholas Kazan (based on book by Alan Dershowitz)
Starring: Jeremy Irons, Glenn Close, Ron Silver

QUESTIONS FOR ACTIVE VIEWING

You are to answer the following questions day by day. Since this assignment is designed to focus your attention on how a narrative (story) is crafted to manipulate your opinions of its main characters through changing points of view and corruption of linear plot structure, it is essential that you follow this requirement. It might be best to take notes on a separate sheet of paper and then draft responses for homework. Make sure you *watch* the film and don't just *listen* to it.

Day One (first forty minutes)

- What visual and sound cues (lighting, camera movement, music) in the opening scenes in the hospital help to establish Sunny's unique perspective as one of the film's narrators?
- How does Sunny's first segment reveal the necessary background information? Jot down the significant details in the order that they are presented.
- What impression do you form of her husband, Claus?
- To what extent do you question the truthfulness of Sunny's account?
- Why is it necessary for the viewer to be aware that Dershowitz is involved in the Johnson brothers' case?
- How does this shape your view of him as a lawyer and a man?
- How do Claus' scenes (there are three throughout the day's viewing) with Dershowitz help to characterize him either as a victim of circumstance or as a morally suspect figure?
- To what extent are we meant to judge Claus through Dershowitz's eyes? Which narratives (plotline, dialogue) or cinematics (visual, sound) suggest this? Which do not?
- What does the flashback involving Maria's testimony establish?
- To what extent does David Marriott appear to be a valuable and credible source of information? On what do you base your judgment?
- To what extent does Sunny's second segment help to establish her as a sympathetic character or not?

End of day one: Is Claus guilty of inflicting the coma on his wife or not? Cite the three most compelling pieces of evidence that the film reveals thus far.

Day Two (40:00–1:16:37)

- How does Claus' macabre sense of humor emerge in the restaurant scene? How does this character trait influence our determination if he is guilty or not?
- How does Claus artfully manipulate the truth in the way he answers (or doesn't answer) Dershowitz's and his students' questions? How does the film's flashback technique become more complex in this day's viewing?
- How do you assess Sunny's version of the comas and their marital difficulties after experiencing Claus' version?
- How do Dershowitz's reactions to Claus color your impression of Claus and his innocence or guilt?
- How does Sunny's segment in this day's viewing mediate your impression of her after her appearances in Claus' versions of the events leading to her comas?
- Which details by the end of this viewing segment start to make Claus emerge as a victim?
- What does the reappearance of David Marriott add to the plotline and your impression of his credibility?

End of day two: Is Claus guilty? Cite the three most compelling details. Has your judgment changed since yesterday? Why or why not?

Day Three (1:16:38 to end)

- Cite an example (or two) of an instance when what Claus is describing doesn't match what is visually revealed in the flashback. At that point, what are we meant to judge as "truthful," the image or the words? Explain your choice.
- Which aspects of Dershowitz's behavior make him, from time to time, morally or legally suspect?
- How are Claus' versions of the events (truth) revised during this day's viewing? Why did he withhold this information earlier?
- What do Sunny's comments leading into the trial scenes help us understand about her and the nature of truth in this situation?
- How do Sara's and Dershowitz's versions of Sunny's second coma help to clarify or mystify the truth? Why "show" what they would normally describe in dialogue?
- How do the following aspects of the end of the film help us to find closure and feel satisfied that we know the "truth" of Claus' guilt or innocence:

  Dershowitz's final words to Claus
  Sunny's final narration of what can be known and unknown
  Claus' comments to the drugstore clerk

Culminating Writing Activity for Reversal of Fortune

Explore how the shifting points of view and narrative structure provide sufficient and satisfying closure to the story. To what extent do you know more or less about the circumstances of Sunny's second coma and Claus' culpability at the end of the film than you did at the beginning? How does the film's structure constantly challenge the viewer's ability to make decisions about the guilt or innocence of Claus von Bülow (considering that the issues of his guilt are still pending in the popular press and the public imagination)? Overall, how satisfying was this experience for you as a viewer? What other films or novels compare in their structure, point of view, and purpose?

When students have finished viewing the film in its entirety, we spend a full class period discussing what is their final "verdict" for Claus and how they constructed that opinion. We cue up scenes (as many as we can) to examine information that is crucial to accepting his innocence or guilt—or more provocatively, never being able to know absolutely if he is guilty or innocent. This models the reading process that is vital to understanding the complex and competing points of view in a text like *The Sound and the Fury*. Most students then become more accustomed to the "healthy pleasure of confusion and disquietude" that an AP prompt once pointed out.

Teachers can use the classic *Citizen Kane*, the Japanese language film *Rashomon*, or a more contemporary film such as *Courage Under Fire* just as effectively to analyze the shifting viewpoints and fractured chronology that is explored in the model study guide for *Reversal of Fortune*.

Mythology

A unit in Greek mythology is a staple in most high school or junior high curricula. A natural way to culminate the study of the heroic journey in classical mythology is to examine how it has been adapted and translated to film. In the years that I taught Greek mythology to accelerated freshmen, I always ended our study with Barry Levinson's film *The Natural*. The students would have read Edith Hamilton's versions of the journeys of both Odysseus and Jason as well as William Saroyan's novel *The Human Comedy*. By that time they were very comfortable with discussing the patterns of characters, incident, and icons in classical and modernized heroic tales. Here are the questions that I provided students to guide their viewing.

The Natural

Direction: Barry Levinson
Screenplay: Roger Towne and Phil Dusenberry
Starring: Robert Redford, Glenn Close, Wilford Brimley, Robert Duvall

Before reviewing the film, discuss in a paragraph how baseball in America has been elevated to a mythic element.

QUESTIONS FOR ACTIVE VIEWING

Roy Hobbs

- How is Roy Hobbs characterized in heroic terms in the prologue of the film?
- Why are details about his childhood and his Midwestern roots so important?
- What elements of the film (visual and narrative) in the beginning help to create the feeling of a modern fairy tale or myth?
- How does Hobbs become a victim of fate?

Visual Details: Look for visual details that help to establish and define forces of good and the forces of evil (or temptation). Note particularly the use of color in costumes and lighting. Cite three specific examples.

Lighting, Film Speed, and Music: Cite three scenes in which the lighting, film speed, or music is used to give Hobbs' return to heroic deeds the fairy-tale, mythic quality of the prologue.

Motif: Why is lightning an important motif in the film? Cite examples of its use in the film and discuss the effectiveness of each example.

Superstition: Describe the role of superstition in one scene or in the development of one character.

Women: The "woman in black," Memo Paris, and Iris resemble which female figures in Greek mythology? Briefly explain your choices.

Antagonist: How is Max Mercy an important link between events and eras depicted in the film? How does he function as an antagonist?

The Ending: Compare the ending of the film with the end of Bernard Malamud's source novel. Identify the differences between the two. Which one is more satisfying to you? Explain your reason. Which of the two endings fits better with developing Hobbs as a mythic hero? Why?

Joseph Campbell: After reading Joseph Campbell's excerpt from *The Power of Myth*, apply the following stages of the monomythic journey to the journey Roy Hobbs takes throughout the course of the film: separation, initiation, conflict, return, boon.

An extension of the viewing and discussion of this film would be to have students locate other texts, both visual and written, that adapt the classic journey of the hero to a modern context. With this kind of application of classical mythology to popular culture texts, students can clearly see how pervasive the literary tradition of an ancient culture is still alive and well.

Satire

Another daunting task for the teacher of literature is helping students understand the techniques of satire and their application in various literary forms. I have used Tim Burton's film *Edward Scissorhands* as an introduction to satire in a senior-year world literature elective that examines Molière's *Tartuffe* as its primary satiric text. Though

Edward Scissorhands is very broad and obvious in its satiric technique, the study of this film will help students identify and apply the basic techniques of satire and refine their understanding of satire during the study of the literature that forms the bulk of the unit.

Edward Scissorhands

Direction: Tim Burton

Screenplay: Caroline Thompson

Starring: Johnny Depp, Winona Ryder, Dianne Wiest, Vincent Price, Alan Arkin

QUESTIONS FOR ACTIVE VIEWING

- With what type of frame does the film open? How does this device prepare the viewer for what is to come? How does it set the tone of the film? How does it later provide resolution?
- To what extent does the film have the quality of a fairy tale or fable?
- How does Edward's first glimpse at suburbia reveal the film's satirical quality? Consider the depiction of the setting as well as Edward's reactions.
- What are the targets of satire in the film? Identify three as the story unfolds.
- To what extent is it important to have a naive outsider reveal the foolish and wicked people in this context?
- Select two characters who are revealed as foolish. What makes them so?
- Which two characters are revealed as wicked or grotesque (other than Edward)? What makes them so?
- Of the four characters that you've selected, which one is presented as a caricature? Which characteristics of this individual are exaggerated? How does the actor portray these exaggerations?
- How are other techniques of satire used in either a visual or verbal manner? Choose three and cite specific examples of hyperbole/overstatement, irony (verbal or situational), sarcasm, incongruity, or understatement.
- To what extent is the situation that Edward finds himself in with his adoptive family absurd, painful, or a combination of both? What contributes to the absurd or painful nature of his situation?
- How is this situation improved by Edward's presence?
- What makes it difficult or impossible for Edward to remain in that situation?
- After viewing the film in its entirety, evaluate the film's effectiveness as a modern example of satire. To what extent is the film's satiric approach caustic or gentle? Explain your choice, citing at least three specific examples. Is the film more effective as a fairy tale or fable? Why or why not?

If there is no time for screening an entire film, David Byrne's *True Stories* provides an episodic format of one man visiting Virgil, Texas, as he investigates the life and times of the important and not-so-important denizens of the town on the occasion of its sesquicentennial. Once again, the targets of Byrne's satire and his techniques are fairly clear—as is the case with *Edward Scissorhands*—and any one or two of the scenes in the film would provide warm-up activities for identifying and discussing the techniques of satire.

Film Companions to Literary Texts

Probably the most effective way to keep a film viewing at the end of the literature unit from becoming a passive experience is to select a companion film to complement the literary text that has been studied. A companion film should treat a similar plot structure or set of character relationships, develop characters in a manner consistent with the literary text, or set the source story in different culture (Akira Kurosawa did this routinely with Shakespeare's works in films like *Throne of Blood* (*Macbeth*) and *Ran* (*King Lear*). Appendix A at the end of this chapter lists a series of film companions to works commonly taught in American, British, and world literature classes. Several companion films and assignments that I have used over the years in my senior literature elective classes for the study of *King Lear*, *Heart of Darkness*, and *Frankenstein* are listed below.

King Lear: Companion Film *The Dresser* (1983)

Direction: Peter Yates
Screenplay: Ronald Harwood (based on his play)
Starring: Albert Finney and Tom Courtenay

The Dresser is a film that loosely draws its characterization of Sir and the title character, Norman, his dresser, on the relationship developed between King Lear and his fool in Shakespeare's tragedy. Sir shares Lear's crumbling mental capacity and Norman cajoles him into brief periods of sanity in the jesting manner of Lear's Fool to help Sir give his final performance of King Lear in a provincial town in WWII-era England.

QUESTIONS FOR ACTIVE VIEWING
- What kind of world has Sir created for himself? How is it deteriorating?
- Who are his enemies in this world? What threat do they pose?
- Why set this story during World War II? How does the war intrude on Sir's world? How does he regard these intrusions? Give examples of how he tries to assert his power over his world and the outside world.
- What role does Norman, Sir's dresser, play in this world? What power does he have? How does he assert it?
- Why is the character of Madge, the stage manager, an important one? What relationship does she have with Sir? How does she regard this relationship?

- How does Madge's character provide contrast to other characters in the company?
- What character traits does Sir share with Lear? Give examples of Sir's behavior that support your choice of traits.
- How does the viewer know that Sir was once great?
- Does Sir act the part of the hero in real life as he does on the stage? Explain.
- How do Norman and Sir share a relationship similar to that of Lear and his Fool?
- How does Norman differ in some respects from the Fool?
- Consider the end of the film. How is it appropriate to the conflict developed here?

Teachers of *King Lear* can also choose to screen and study Akira Kurosawa's *Ran*, set in Japan's samurai culture; Edward Dmytryk's western adaptation, *Broken Lance*; or Jocelyn Moorhouse's film version of Jane Smiley's novel *A Thousand Acres*, which sets the tragedy in modern Iowa. The questions developed for *The Dresser* can certainly serve as a model for these films to focus students' viewing on a critical analysis of the adaptation.

Heart of Darkness: Companion Film *Apocalypse Now* (1979)

Direction: Francis Ford Coppola
Screenplay: Francis Ford Coppola and John Milius
Starring: Marlon Brando, Robert Duvall, Martin Sheen, Sam Bottoms, Dennis Hopper, Larry Fishburne

Probably the most well-known companion film to a classic literary work is Francis Ford Coppola's epic film *Apocalypse Now*. As much praised as maligned, the film graphically imagines the horror of Vietnam and Cambodia through the anti-imperialistic lens of Joseph Conrad's *Heart of Darkness*. It is a difficult film to watch. As with all films of this nature, it is recommended that both administrative and parental permission be sought prior to screening the film in class.

QUESTIONS FOR ACTIVE VIEWING
- How does the opening montage of images and sounds set the tone of the film?
- How is Willard depicted in the initial scenes (before he receives his mission)? What explanation seems to be offered for his behavior?
- What type of information does Willard receive about Kurtz during the briefing on the mission? What impression does Willard form of Kurtz? How does that impression change or develop as he goes up river?
- How is this characterization of Kurtz similar to or different from the one Marlow acquires in the novel?
- What makes Willard "suitable" for this mission?

- Describe the men on the boat with Willard, listed below. What types of soldiers do they represent? Identify a critical event that changes each man and/or Willard's attitude toward him.

  Chef

  Lance

  Mr. Clean

  Chief Phillips

- Describe the major characters that Willard meets as he goes up river. What is each man preoccupied with?
- How do the characters listed view the war? The Vietnamese? How does Willard view them?

  Kilgore

  the photographer

  Colby

- As Willard moves up river, which events influence him most? Which plot elements of the river trip correspond to the novel? Why do you think Coppola retained these events?
- Which key events and/or characters are missing that you feel were vital to the development of the novel? Explain why you think each was omitted. (Identify at least two.)
- How is the poetry of T. S. Eliot incorporated into the latter parts of the film? How is it appropriately (or pretentiously) used? How does its use point toward a theme?
- Discuss how the meeting between Kurtz and Willard is expanded from the contact that Kurtz and Marlow have in the novel. How are both characters depicted differently at this point in the film than they were depicted in the novel? (Is it simply expanding the role to suit Brando's star status?)
- How does Brando's physical and vocal characterization of Kurtz fit with how this character is depicted in the novel? How do lighting and camerawork help depict the emotional and psychological aspects of the character?
- How is the element of the native woman, who is depicted in the novel, handled in the film? What meaning does her presence have?
- How is the execution of Kurtz depicted through use of a visual metaphor?
- How satisfying and appropriate is the ending of the film?

To culminate the study of Conrad's novel reimagined in Vietnam, view the documentary film *Hearts of Darkness: A Filmmaker's Apocalypse.* Coppola's wife, Eleanor, shot the award-winning film that was only assembled and released in 1991. It may not be possible to screen the entire film, but the opening section on Orson Welles' failed attempt to bring a faithful adaptation of Conrad's novel to the screen before *Citizen Kane* is particularly useful in understanding the difficulty of adapting a literary text into a cinematic form. The study of *Apocalypse Now* would not be complete without a screening of Ernie Fosselius' twenty-minute parody, "Porklips Now."

Frankenstein: Companion Films

The inclusion of companion films should not be limited to screening in class. If students have had some training in the careful analysis of a filmic text, study of companion films can and should be offered as part of the essay topics offered at the end of a unit of study. Here are some sample topics that I have used after completing the study of Mary Shelley's *Frankenstein*. The first two topics are relatively routine, focusing on the analysis of a traditional cinematic adaptation of the novel. The other two topics offer films that are in the vein of the film companion and films that are loosely based on or connected to characters, situations, or themes depicted in the novel.

WRITING/VIEWING ASSIGNMENTS

- View the two film versions of *Frankenstein* (both are roughly seventy minutes long) created in the 1930s, *Frankenstein* and *Bride of Frankenstein*, and discuss how and why Hollywood has changed Mary Shelley's concept of the creature and his creator as well as plot elements. How do these changes alter the viewer's perception of both characters?

- Screen Kenneth Branagh's most recent version, *Mary Shelley's Frankenstein*, promoted as a faithful adaptation of Shelley's novel. Select three scenes or sequences from the film and discuss how each scene remains true to the spirit and composition of the original or makes changes that enhance or detract from the original source material's intent. You may want to research some reviews of the film or read Branagh's introduction (he directs the film and plays Victor) to the published film script. You could choose to use another adaptation of the novel, but be careful. There are over one hundred adaptations, some good, but many that are really awful and have little to do with the novel. Clear an alternate choice with your teacher.

- A very different option would be to watch *Blade Runner*, a sci-fi film that deals with a future society that creates an underclass of "replicants." If you should choose this option, here is one approach to analyze it: Examine why this future society has chosen to create this class of replicants. What are the pros and cons of having these "creatures" be a part of this society from the point of view of their creator, a common citizen, and the replicants? Is there any other "underclass" other than the replicants? How are they treated similarly or differently? What process was used to bring them to life? Compare and contrast it to the "science" used in the novel. What relationship do these creatures have with their creators? humans? with other replicants? Compare and contrast the emotional nature of the replicants and the extent to which they suffer conflicts with Shelley's creature. Find other connections between this very modern film (ahead of its time cinematically and narratively) and Shelley's romantic novel (ahead of its time as well). Can a sci-fi film tap into any or all of the themes/concerns of the romantic age?

- Compare and contrast the character of Carl from *Sling Blade* with the creature in *Frankenstein*. How have Carl's experiences in an institution and his upbringing by his parents contributed to his dehumanization? How are his experiences outside of the institution similar to the humanizing process of the creature? How does Carl have aspirations and desires that are similar to the creature's? How are his aggressive and violent impulses brought out in ways similar to those depicted in the novel? Note the song that plays over the credits at the end of the film. How does it address some of the themes or ideas related to the similarities between Carl and the creature?

The study of film can bring together a variety of viewing, speaking, writing, and critical thinking skills that can be a substantial instructional meal in itself and not just a confection. With thought, preparation, and careful execution, its integration into a literature curriculum can offer extraordinary enrichment potential for students of all abilities.

Films Cited

Feature-Length Films

Apocalypse Now, 1979, Francis Ford Coppola, R, 153 min.

Blade Runner, 1982, Ridley Scott, R, 114 min.

Bride of Frankenstein, 1935, James Whale, NR, 73 min.

Broken Lance, 1954, Edward Dmytryk, NR, 96 min.

Citizen Kane, 1941, Orson Welles, NR, 120 min.

Courage Under Fire, 1996, Edward Zwick, R, 115 min.

The Dresser, 1983, Peter Yates, R, 118 min.

Edward Scissorhands, 1990, Tim Burton, PG, 100 min.

The 400 Blows, 1959, Francois Truffaut, NR, 93 min.

Frankenstein, 1931, James Whale, NR, 71 min.

Great Expectations, 1946, David Lean, NR, 118 min.

Hearts of Darkness: A Filmmaker's Apocalypse, 1991, Eleanor Coppola, R, 96 min.

Looking for Richard, 1996, Al Pacino, PG13, 109 min.

Mary Shelley's Frankenstein, 1994, Kenneth Branagh, R, 123 min.

The Natural, 1984, Barry Levinson, PG, 134 min.

Rashomon, 1950, Akira Kurosawa, NR, 83 min.

Reversal of Fortune, 1990, Barbet Schroeder, R, 110 min.

Shakespeare in Love, 1998, John Madden, R, 122 min.

Sling Blade, 1996, Billy Bob Thornton, R, 136 min.

Small Change, 1976, Francois Truffaut, NR, 105 min.

A Thousand Acres, 1997, Jocelyn Moorhouse, R, 105 min.

True Stories, 1986, David Byrne, PG, 90 min.

Episodic Television

"A Modern Prometheus," *The X-Files*, 1997, 10 Thirteen Productions, 47 min.

Short Subject Films

Discovering Hamlet, 1990, PBS Video, 53 min.

The Great Books series, 1990s–ongoing, The Discovery Channel, 30 min.

"Porklips Now," *Hardware Wars and Other Parodies*, 1978, Warner Video, 20 min.

Shakespeare: The Animated Tales, 1992, Random House Video, 30 min.

Shakespeare in the Classroom, 1999, Miramax, 45 min.

Silent Shakespeare, 1999, BFI/Milestone Video, 88 min.

"The True Story of Frankenstein," 1994, A&E Network, 100 min.

Understanding Shakespeare: The Tragedies, 1993, Goldhill Video, 90 min.

"William Shakespeare: A Concise Biography," 1992, *Famous Authors* series, 30 min.

"William Shakespeare: Life in Drama," 1996, A&E *Biography*, 50 min.

Resource List of Companion Films to Literature

American Literature

Angela's Ashes	*The Butcher Boy* (R)	Neil Jordan
	This Is My Father (R)	Paul Quinn
	The Secret of Roan Inish	John Sayles
	The McCourts of Limerick (documentary)	Conor McCourt
The Awakening	*My Brilliant Career*	Gillian Armstrong
The Crucible	*Guilty by Suspicion*	Irwin Winkler
	On the Waterfront	Elia Kazan
The Elephant Man	*My Left Foot*	Jim Sheridan
Farewell to Manzanar	*Come See the Paradise*	Alan Parker

	Rabbit in the Moon (documentary)	Emiko Omori
	Beyond the Barbed Wire (documentary)	Steve Rosen
The Great Gatsby	*Citizen Kane*	Orson Welles
	Six Degrees of Separation	Fred Schepisi
The Joy Luck Club	*A Great Wall*	Peter Wang
My Antonia	*Days of Heaven*	Terrence Malick
✓*One Flew Over the Cuckoo's Nest*	*Cool Hand Luke*	Stuart Rosenberg
Our Town	*Shadow of a Doubt* (script by Thornton Wilder)	Alfred Hitchcock
A Raisin in the Sun	*The Long Walk Home*	Richard Pearce
A Separate Peace	*Dead Poets Society*	Peter Weir
	School Ties	Robert Mandel
	Chariots of Fire	Hugh Hudson
To Kill a Mockingbird	*Places in the Heart*	Robert Benton
The Woman Warrior	*A Thousand Pieces of Gold*	Nancy Kelly
	Raise the Red Lantern (R)	Zhang Yimou

British Literature

Beowulf (the questing hero)	*Raiders of the Lost Ark*	Steven Spielberg
	The Searchers	John Ford
	Star Wars	George Lucas
Emma	*Clueless*	Amy Heckerling
	Cold Comfort Farm	John Schlesinger
Frankenstein	*Edward Scissorhands*	Tim Burton
	Blade Runner (R)	Ridley Scott
	Sling Blade (R)	Billy Bob Thornton
	Young Frankenstein	Mel Brooks
Gilgamesh	*Star Trek: The Next Generation,* "Darmok"	Winrich Kolbe
Hamlet	*The Last Action Hero*	John McTiernan
	Rosencrantz and Guildenstern Are Dead	Tom Stoppard
	A Midwinter's Tale	Kenneth Branagh
	Royal Deceit (R)	Gabriel Axel
	The Lion King	Roger Allers and Rob Minkoff

Heart of Darkness	Apocalypse Now (R)	Francis Ford Coppola
	Lord Jim	Richard Brooks
	The Mission (R)	Roland Joffé
	Farewell to the King	John Milius
Henry IV & Henry V	My Own Private Idaho (R)	Gus Van Sant
	Chimes at Midnight	Orson Welles
Jane Eyre	Rebecca	Alfred Hitchcock
King Lear	The Dresser	Peter Yates
	Ran (R)	Akira Kurosawa
	Lear	Jean-Luc Godard
	A Thousand Acres (R)	Jocelyn Moorhouse
Macbeth	Throne of Blood	Akira Kurosawa
	Men of Respect (R)	William Reilly
	Fury Is a Woman (aka Siberian Lady Macbeth)	Andrej Wadia
Othello	A Double Life	George Cukor
Pygmalion	She's All That	Robert Iscove
Romeo and Juliet	Zebrahead (R)	Anthony Drazan
	Solomon and Gaenor (R)	Paul Morrison
Silas Marner	A Simple Twist of Fate	Gillies MacKinnon
Sir Gawain and the Green Knight	Ladyhawke	Richard Donner
The Taming of the Shrew	10 Things I Hate About You	Gil Junger
The Tempest	Forbidden Planet	Fred McLeod Wilcox
	Tempest (R)	Paul Mazursky
	Prospero's Books (NC-17)	Peter Greenaway
Waiting for Godot	La Strada	Frederico Fellini
	Rosencrantz and Guildenstern Are Dead	Tom Stoppard

World Literature

All Quiet on the Western Front	Gallipoli	Peter Weir
	Paths of Glory	Stanley Kubrick
	A Midnight Clear (R)	Keith Gordon
Crime and Punishment	Compulsion	Richard Fleischer
	In Cold Blood	Richard Brooks
	Crimes and Misdemeanors	Woody Allen

	Crime and Punishment in Suburbia (R)	Rob Schmidt
Cyrano de Bergerac	Roxanne	Fred Schepisi
	Whatever It Takes	David Raynr
	The Truth About Cats and Dogs	Michael Lehmann
Dante's Inferno	Seven (R)	David Fincher
	The Ninth Gate (R)	Roman Polanski
	What Dreams May Come	Vincent Ward
A Doll House	My Brilliant Career	Gillian Armstrong
	The Official Story	Luis Puenzo
Fathers and Sons	Death of a Salesman (Hoffman version)	Volker Schlöndorff
Les Miserables	Les Miserables (WWII setting)	Claude Lelouche
Master Harold and 'the boys'	A World Apart	Chris Menges
	A World of Strangers	Henning Carlson
	The Power of One	John G. Avildsen
The Metamorphosis	Franz Kafka's It's a Wonderful Life	Peter Capaldi
	Kafka	Steven Soderbergh
Nectar in a Sieve	City of Joy	Roland Joffé
	Pather Panchali	Satyajit Ray
Night	Empire of the Sun	Steven Spielberg
	Au Revoir, Les Enfants	Louis Malle
Notes From the Underground	Taxi Driver (R)	Martin Scorsese
Oedipus Rex	"Oedipus Wrecks" from New York Stories	Woody Allen
	Mighty Aphrodite (Greek Chorus scenes)	Woody Allen
The Odyssey	Oh Brother, Where Art Thou (R)	Coen Brothers
Uncle Vanya	Country Life	Michael Blakemore
	Vanya on 42nd Street	Louis Malle

SEVEN

Making Connections: Literary Themes in Film

ELLEN KRUEGER

They should make this into a movie!
(STUDENT GREG, AFTER READING FLANNERY O'CONNOR'S "A GOOD MAN IS
HARD TO FIND")

Modern American Writers is a one-semester elective offered in my department that provides an in-depth study of twentieth-century fiction and drama. The course focuses on the works of authors who have received both popular and critical acclaim. Traditionally, the course is taught chronologically, recommending titles by Fitzgerald, Hemingway, and Parker in the 1920s; Lillian Hellman in the 1930s; Tennessee Williams and Arthur Miller in the 1940s; Roth, Cheever, and O'Connor in the 1950s; and Wasserstein in the 1980s. After teaching the course for many years, I decided to organize the course thematically and to add a film component. According to one of the NCTE tenets of media literacy, students need to construct meaning through different media and analyze their transactions with media texts. Although including film means teaching fewer titles and authors, I think making connections between literature and film is extremely worthwhile. Using film is another way to foster critical thinking skills.

The objectives of the course lend themselves equally to film and to literature. For example, if we examine literary techniques such as point of view, symbolism, imagery, theme, and style in novels, plays, and short stories, then we can also examine film conventions such as framing, placement, arrangement, lighting, color, sound, and editing in the movies we see. The emphasis of the course leans more heavily toward stylistic and thematic literary analysis, but students learn very quickly how a director makes a story cinematic while conveying a vision. Just as a writer must pick and choose his words carefully to deliver his ideas, so, too, must the film crew arrange, compose, and edit to convey the desired effect. The possibilities in connecting literature and film study are too rich to ignore.

The Western: A Truly American Genre

Since we will be reading a variety of literary genres, and since I want to prepare my students for the visual component of the course, I like to begin with a short introduction to America's most distinctive narrative form and enduring genre of films, the western. Westerns make serious use of the physical landscapes, whether in Monument Valley or small towns; a colorful cast of characters, such as heroes, villains, outlaws, saloon singers, and loners; and recognizable images, such as horses, guns, clothing, and stagecoaches. They are generally presented in a conventional narrative structure, and are richly endowed with themes exploring honor and integrity, life and death, and good and evil. The western contributes as much to our national identity and our cultural heritage as do the works of twentieth-century authors.

Clips from John Ford's *Stagecoach* or *My Darling Clementine*, Fred Zinnemann's *High Noon*, or George Stevens' *Shane* will provide students with a chance to experience the conventions of the western as well as with an orientation to the conventions of filmmaking.

Stagecoach, which is often considered the quintessential western, is the one I use. The film opens in Tonto, Arizona, where preparation is being made for a stagecoach ride to Lordsburg, New Mexico. Here we meet the passengers, a recognizable group of stock characters: the kindhearted fallen woman, the southern gambler, the alcoholic doctor, the corrupt banker, the prim army wife, and the meek whiskey salesman. Once the stagecoach leaves town, it is stopped by the Ringo Kid (John Wayne), a cowboy outlaw who has busted out of the penitentiary to seek revenge against the Plummer boys, who gunned down his father and brother. Together, the group continues en route to Lordsburg, paying little heed to the warning of attacks from Geronimo and the Apaches. After the setting, cast, and conflict are established, we turn our attention to how the story relies on cinematography to make it come alive for us.

Since the landscape of the West is so essential to the genre, I tell my students that most westerns were filmed on location in Texas, Wyoming, or Montana. *Stagecoach* was filmed in Monument Valley, Utah, where the broad open spaces provided a dramatic backdrop for the action. After a short lesson on basic film terminology, we begin to watch the opening sequence announcing the credits. I ask my students what they notice about the camerawork, the use of black-and-white film, and the sounds. With minimal formal training, they are able to identify extreme long shots of Monument Valley filmed at a high angle. A stagecoach rides through the valley floor, passing mesas and rock outcroppings, kicking up dust, as the camera captures the beauty and barrenness of the land. I always ask them to identify what they are feeling as they are watching. They realize how the positioning of the camera dwarfs the stagecoach and shows its vulnerability against the natural elements. Another long shot shows the Apaches sitting on horseback, shot in silhouette, as they watch the movement below from on top of a hill. Accompanied by an ominous drumbeat, the students recognize this as foreshadowing. They notice that the camera is much closer when the passengers are introduced to the story, which we identify as a medium shot. Each character's identity is revealed from a shot taken at arm's length. When the Ringo Kid enters the story, the camera zooms slowly into a close-up of him as he twirls his Winchester. He wears the traditional garb of the cowboy—bandanna, hat, jeans, and boots. We can tell from his face and manner that he's a good guy. We also discuss the use of black-and-white film. Students agree that the drab colors reinforce a bygone era in which ordinary people struggle to survive against the rustic environment. In terms of music, the upbeat, fast-paced sounds of the cavalry riding their horses across the valley as they approach town are easily contrasted to the ominous drumbeats of Indians lying in wait on horseback. We discuss the choices Ford made, scene by scene, to make the story come alive for the audience.

Using the western as a brief introduction to a course on American literature serves several purposes. First, it exposes today's student population to a genre that is all but forgotten or ignored due to preferences for other genres. Although other genres have replaced the western, none has provided such a rich reflection of our national history and identity. Second, studying westerns is helpful for understanding the American landscape and the American characters who populate contemporary fiction. Third, experiencing westerns establishes aesthetic connections between literature and film. Enduring themes such as family, authority, morality, social justice, violence, codes of behavior, romanticism, freedom, adventure, idealism, and wanderlust, which were inherent in westerns, are still essential elements in modern literature. Comparing and contrasting themes and conventions will continue throughout the following units.

The American Dream

Just as codes of behavior were important to the cowboy living in the untamed wilds of the frontier, contemporary characters in fiction and film must wrestle with similar codes. However, the enemies are no longer Indians or outlaws, but rather a system of values or beliefs. This conflict is evoked in a statement made by Ben Younger, director of *Boiler Room*: "But where do you draw the line between greed and wanting to live a better life and the American dream?" Younger's question reinforces the unifying theme of one of my units in the Modern American Writers course: The American Dream/Nightmare.

The three texts I use for this unit are: *The Great Gatsby* (a novel) by F. Scott Fitzgerald, *Death of a Salesman* (a play) by Arthur Miller, and *Wall Street* (a film), directed by Oliver Stone. These selections address the need for students to construct meaning through different media as they analyze their transactions with these texts. I want my students to make thematic connections regarding the American dream in several different genres. Throughout the twentieth century, one recurrent theme in literature and film, from Theodore Dreiser's *An American Tragedy* to Robert Zemeckis' *Forrest Gump*, is the journey from rags to riches. Using the three texts mentioned above, we examine what happens as these characters forge ahead blindly in pursuit of the dream. Jay Gatsby, Willy Loman, and Bud Fox placed tremendous emphasis on achieving extrinsic goals of being financially successful and being well-liked.

As an overview, it might be helpful to review the many qualities that connect these three texts. Among them are the east coast settings. In *Gatsby* and *Salesman*, the West also plays a significant role. They all involve complex relationships between fathers and sons or surrogate fathers and young men. With the exception of Linda Loman, the portrayal of women is less than flattering. All three texts make strong use of symbolism. Thematically, they address the corrupting influence of money on human values, and the loss of values that results from pursuing the wrong dreams.

I always show the film after we have read and written about the literature. In this way, students are applying critical thinking skills with which they are familiar—comprehension, analysis, synthesis, and evaluation—to the film, while adding the new cinematic perspective. With every film I show my students, I prepare a series of active viewing questions designed to address the issues I want them to notice. In this case, I want them to notice the style of the filmmaker, the ways in which characters, settings, and themes are developed cinematically, and their roles as viewers. After the viewing, we will draw comparisons with the literature to determine how words and images differ, and how the roles of readers and viewers differ.

Questions to Promote Active Viewing

The following are the types of viewing questions I've designed for *Wall Street*, with commentary that might be used for discussion.

1. F. Scott Fitzgerald used lyrical language to establish his Long Island settings. Arthur Miller used theatrical conventions to establish his New York and Boston settings. How does Oliver Stone establish his New York settings in the opening scenes of the film?

   After analyzing the language and stage craft of Fitzgerald and Miller, it is time to turn to the structural techniques of filmmaking. Briefed before the film with a lesson in basic film terminology during the unit on the western, my students have no difficulty identifying how the camera establishes downtown Manhattan during rush hour. They follow the camera movement as it captures images of the Fulton Fish Market, the New York skyline, the Staten Island ferry, F.D.R. Drive, the Brooklyn Bridge, the New York Stock Exchange, and shots of subways, skyscrapers, crowded sidewalks, traffic, and packed elevators. While we're watching this montage of images from aerial shots, long shots, and pan shots, we hear Frank Sinatra, the quintessential New Yorker, sing "Fly Me to the Moon." Clearly, Stone doesn't need dialogue or voice-over to establish the rat race of early morning commuter life.

2. How is Bud Fox's character introduced?

   Similar to fiction writers and dramatists, a filmmaker uses action and dialogue to reveal characterization. We watch Bud as he begins his day riding the elevator up to the brokerage firm where he works. The camera follows his movements as he begins his day, cold calling leads. Based on dialogue and interaction with others, Bud's character begins to evolve. Although raised in a modest middle-class family, he is a bright, ambitious young man who is eager to advance as a stock broker.

3. We learned things about Jay Gatsby before we met him. What do we learn about Gordon Gekko before we meet him? after we meet him?

   Dialogue serves to characterize Gordon Gekko. Our perceptions are also formed by the comments of others. We learn that Gekko made several multimillion-dollar deals before he was forty, just as Gatsby came into great wealth as a young man. Rumors about these men abound as well. Both seem to have made their fortunes through questionable means, whether bootlegging or insider trading. Mystery and intrigue surround them. When Bud finally meets Gekko, the camera pans his impressive office, which contains canvases of modern art, floor-to-ceiling windows with a view of Manhattan, computer terminals, and a blood pressure machine. Unlike Gatsby, Gekko functions at a frenetic pace. He carries on multiple conversations, entertains phone calls, and allows Bud a few moments of his time to ingratiate himself. Close-up shots of Gekko's face convey an aggressive, impatient, demanding nature. He even smokes a cigarette while he takes his blood pressure.

4. Both Gatsby and Gekko entertain at their homes on Long Island. How does Stone use this scene to continue to develop Gekko's character?

   Stone arranges and composes his shots to create the world of the nouveau riche. The house is ultra-modern, decorated with expensive furniture, rugs, paintings, sculptures, and accessories. The camera captures Bud's face as he reacts, in awe of this environment. The living room is populated with young, beautiful, and trendy people. However, eavesdropping on their conversations about bikini waxes and infidelities, we learn how superficial they are, just as we did while listening to dialogues between Gatsby's guests. Both Gatsby and Gekko continue to conduct business throughout the duration of the evening.

5. Bud's financial success affords him the opportunity of moving to the Upper East Side, a posh address. The renovation of his apartment is shown through a series of images—a montage—accompanied by surreal-sounding music. What feeling is Stone trying to convey?

   Stone arranges shots of false brick being glued to the wall, artificial gold leafing applied to the molding, and balloon shades affixed to the windows, while the lyrics of the song suggest "home is where I want to be." The decor is garish and artificial, but the look is fashionable and expensive. The sequence of shots is disturbing because it reveals Bud's growing materialistic values as he acquires wealth illegally.

6. What do you notice about the final sequence of the film beginning in Central Park and ending on the steps of the court house?

   Stone uses the camera dramatically in both scenes. Bud and Gekko have a showdown in the park, one of the few scenes that take place outdoors, away from the wheeling and dealing of Wall Street. From a long shot, it looks as if Bud and Gordon are meeting on a dreary battlefield. The wide expanse of land is surrounded by towering skyscrapers. Thunder accompanies the meeting, which reinforces Gekko's wrath after he finds out that Bud has "sandbagged" him. In a medium shot, Gordon slugs Bud and delivers a tirade about all he has done for the young man. "I look at you and see myself," to which Bud responds, "I'm just Bud Fox. As much as I wanted to be Gordon Gekko, I'll always be Bud Fox." The final scene of the film shows Bud turning himself in to the authorities. The camera zooms out to an extreme long shot of him climbing the steps of the court house. Bud is reduced to a speck amidst thousands of people on the streets of New York. His crime of committing insider trading is perhaps one of many committed on a single day in any big city anywhere in the world. Stone leaves us with this feeling as the final credits roll.

Post-Viewing Questions

After viewing the film and commenting on the cinematic qualities associated with storytelling, the next step is to make more in-depth connections to the literature. The following list represents a sample of the discussion questions I use.

1. In what ways are Nick Carraway, Biff Loman, and Bud Fox alike? different?

2. Examine the roles of the fathers: Henry Gatz, Willy Loman, and Carl Fox. What impact do they have on their sons' lives? What roles do the surrogate fathers, Dan Cody, Meyer Wolfsheim, Ben, and Gordon Gekko, have on the men in the film?

3. With what values are the characters imbued? Where do you draw the line between greed and the pursuit of the American dream? How does it become destroyed and turn into the nightmare?

4. With what moral dilemmas are Nick, Biff, and Bud faced? How do they resolve them?

5. Contrast Jay Gatsby to Gordon Gekko in terms of their backgrounds, ambitions, dreams, values, and blindness.

6. Examine the roles of the women who are wives (Daisy, Linda, Kate) and girlfriends (Myrtle, Jordan, woman in Boston, Darien).

7. Contrast Gatsby's speech on re-creating the past, Willy's on Dave Singleman, and Gordon's on greed. How do these speeches reveal the illusions of these men?

8. Compare the Valley of Ashes in *The Great Gatsby* to the "abyss" in *Wall Street*. What do Nick and Bud finally see?

9. What does the future hold for Nick, Biff, and Bud?
10. How do author, playwright, and director manipulate symbols? Consider: the green light, Dr. T. J. Eckleberg's eyes, Willy's sample cases, nylon stockings, fountain pen, seed packets, geckos, and Wall Street.

Topics for Essay Writing

The following is a list of topics from which the students may choose to write an essay for their final evaluation. These topics require analysis, synthesis, and evaluation. One is to be selected as the topic of a formal comparison/contrast essay.

1. Complex emotional and psychological father/son relationships are a dominant theme in literature, drama, and film. Compare and contrast the relationships of Henry and Jay, Willy and Biff, and Carl and Bud. Use concrete references to the texts.
2. Gatsby, Willy, and Gordon all believed in the American dream and chased it blindly, only to be destroyed by it. Discuss the similarities and differences among these three characters. Point to specific examples from the texts.
3. Nick, Biff, and Bud all experience "awakenings" at the end of their respective stories. What are they, and how are they similar and different?
4. What makes the experiences of a novel, a play, and a film similar and different for you as a reader and a viewer? Discuss this issue in relation to *The Great Gatsby*, *Death of a Salesman*, and *Wall Street*.

Question number four is the one that most addresses the value of using media in a traditional literature class. The following are excerpts from a student who has successfully articulated the similarities and differences of being a reader and a viewer.

Regina comments on her experiences of the novel: "The medium with which I associate the most is the novel. It is the most unique because it rests completely upon the workings of my imagination. The book that the author creates, no matter how descriptive and detailed, still cannot function without my input. For the words function as the skeleton and the reader must fill in the flesh. For example, when the reader first meets Jay Gatsby, the image he creates is different for each reader despite having read the same words. This is why I like the novel the most. The creation of the characters and the plot relies completely upon the relationship that exists between the words immortalized by the author and me. As a result, I truly feel as if I own the novel because I experienced it."

Next, she contrasts her role as a reader to that of a viewer of a play and a movie. "Though the means by which I experience plays and movies are the same because the creative choices have already been made for me, there are still some differences. The very fact that the actors are performing live in front of me gives me an instant connection with the characters as if their emotions are tangible and I can grab onto them. Something in the air allows me to understand every word and sentiment that the characters are trying to express, and I am able to have a greater level of identification with each character. Like Biff in *Death of a Salesman*, I am horribly exasperated with this old man who is unable to let go of his illusions and face reality. However, I can also relate to Willy because I still hold onto the hope he has for Biff. Finally, during the requiem, every emotion that Linda feels in that small body of hers seems to have been lifted from her body and placed into mine, for it certainly felt as if I was at that funeral mourning Willy's death."

Finally, she explains her experience of viewing a film. "When I sit down to watch a movie, I need to have absolute silence so I can focus all of my attention on the screen in front of me. I attempt to immerse myself in the plot of the story as much as possible, because I feel very removed from what is happening. The movie goes on without me, and all of the details such as music, setting, and costumes have already been arranged according to someone else's vision. My only job is to attempt to comprehend the images that were created and hopefully try to associate with some part of the movie. However, even though I am often unable to connect with the characters' situations, I involuntarily begin to experience similar emotions, which allow me to identify with the character. For example, although the movie *Wall Street* describes a world very different from mine, as the movie progresses, and I learn more about the story and characters from the images on the screen, I begin to feel some of the emotions that Bud feels. When he experiences the demise of his career, I felt sad, frustrated, and also relieved because it put an end to his moral dilemma." Regina concludes that as a reader and a viewer, "I also hope I will be moved emotionally, and ultimately learn more about myself, in addition to being entertained."

Examining the pursuit of the American dream in literature and film forces us to reevaluate our own ethics and to question the price we pay for personal satisfaction. To what degree do affluence and attractiveness contribute to our well-being? What is sacrificed in the pursuit of extrinsic goals? Perhaps the price is the dark side of the American dream: lack of personal honesty, the inability to shed illusions and face the truth, and moral bankruptcy. Making thematic connections between literature and film raises consciousness and fosters critical thinking.

"The Sorrows of Affluence"

In the second unit titled "The Sorrows of Affluence" (borrowed from the title of a film review of *Ordinary People* by Vincent Canby), the texts I've used are *Goodbye, Columbus*, a novella by Philip Roth, *The Stories of John Cheever*, by John Cheever, and *Ordinary People*, a film directed by Robert Redford. The common thematic element shared by all these texts is the dysfunction that hides behind closed doors in upper-middle-class suburban America. Reflecting on the TV images presented to us across the decades, from Ozzie and Harriet Nelson to Rob and Laura Petrie to Carol and Mike Brady to Cliff and Claire Huxtable to Dan and Roseanne Connor, we see media constructions of American families. Unlike those generally happy, well-adjusted families, those that inhabit the pages of postwar fiction challenge that image. The suburban landscapes created by Roth, Cheever, and Redford include country clubs, cocktail parties, golf tournaments, and commuter platforms. These writers explore the lifestyles and values of the ordinary people living respectable, middle-class lives in manicured suburban communities.

Once again, the focus of this unit is to strengthen critical thinking skills (clarifying, questioning, and predicting) as students transact with various media texts. After reading the novella and the stories and conducting a thorough stylistic and thematic analysis of Roth and Cheever, we turn to the film, *Ordinary People*, to continue our study of how a filmmaker tells a story cinematically.

Questions to Promote Active Viewing: Ordinary People

Guided viewing questions are essential for they help raise student awareness of the cinematic qualities of the film. Students must practice how to process information based on visual images and sounds. The following questions and guides represent a sampling of those that I use to help generate discussion.

1. What information is revealed in the opening sequence of the film? Pay attention to the silence in the beginning, followed by piano music, vocal accompaniment, and images with no dialogue. What do you notice about the setting and the characters?

   The camera focuses on the quiet beauty of Lake Michigan, then shows the properties that border the lake in a tree-lined neighborhood where it's very quiet. One impressive-looking house designed in perfect symmetry is singled out by the camera, suggesting an upper-middle-class suburb. The camera then cuts to a shot of Conrad, the teenage protagonist, who is abruptly awakened as if from a nightmare, sitting up in his bed, breathing heavily. From here, the next shot shows his parents who are at the theatre with friends. This sequence of shots, when edited together, clearly establish the setting, the characters, the socioeconomic trappings, and the feeling that something is disturbing the young man's sleep, of which his parents may be unaware.

2. Notice the juxtaposition of images (editing) in the breakfast scene. We see Conrad in his bedroom, Beth and Calvin in the kitchen, Conrad again in his room, and his parents in the kitchen. What effect does this sequence have? How are the family dynamics revealed when Conrad joins them?

   When Conrad is called for breakfast, he appears to be very anxious about something, and calls out in a forced cheerfulness, "be right there!" He joins them in the kitchen, and Beth serves him French toast. When he claims he isn't hungry, Beth removes the meal, as if insulted by his lack of appetite, and throws it down the garbage disposal, claiming, "you can't save French toast." Her behavior seems like an overreaction. Calvin, who is much more concerned with Conrad, makes small talk about getting tickets to a game and asks whether Con has called the doctor yet. Beth leaves the room to get ready for golf. The scene is riddled with tension.

3. Later that night when the family sits down for dinner, notice the seating arrangement, the conversation, and the overall family dynamics.

   Calvin is sitting at the head of the table in between his wife and his son. The camera frames the three of them at the table as they engage in small talk about the fish, the mechanic, and the party Saturday night at the Murray's. The only attention Beth pays to Conrad is to ask him if his shirt is ripped and whether he wants her to sign him up for "round-robin" at the club. Again, Calvin is the one who asks if Con is okay and if he's thought about calling the doctor. The lighting is dim in this very formal setting. Once again, the tension is palpable.

4. In the first flashback, how are lighting, sound, and editing manipulated?

   When the scene flashes back to the boating accident, the lighting is low key and focuses on blue, black, and gray images of the sailboat being violently tossed around in the storm. The camera cuts to Conrad, who is thrashing around in bed, then cuts back to the chaos of the storm. The past is clearly intruding upon the present.

5. Sometimes, silence can be just as powerful as sound. Describe Beth's visit to Buck's room. Notice how the camera controls what we see.

   As Beth hesitantly enters her deceased son's room, the camera pans the walls and shelves showing trophies, posters, pennants, sports equipment, numerous photographs, and an empty twin bed. Obviously, Buck was an exceptional young athlete. His room appears to be a shrine to his memory. The camera shows Beth's sad, distraught face in a dramatic close-up shot.

6. During one of Conrad's sessions with Dr. Berger, notice the lighting. How is Conrad's face captured by the camera?

   The camera illuminates only one side of his face while the other remains in the shadows. This image reflects the conflict that Conrad is experiencing as he tries to understand his tormented emotions surrounding his brother's death. He is wrestling with his guilt, his anger, and his having survived the boating accident. The semi-lit scene shows the slow progress he is making as he responds to therapy.

7. Conrad discovers some very disturbing news about his friend Karen. Closely follow the sequence of events, paying attention to the camerawork, the editing, the sound, and the lighting.

   When Con discovers that Karen has killed herself, he is terribly shaken. He goes into the bathroom, fills the sink with water, and places his hands, wrists facing upward, under the faucet. The camera shows the scarred wrists in a close-up shot. The vertical lines drawn by the razor blade show how serious he was about attempting to take his own life. The sound of the running water perhaps triggers the tragedy he has been trying so desperately to suppress. Then he grabs his jacket and runs out of the house. As he is running wildly through the darkness, he experiences flashbacks of the boating accident. He and Buck are frantically trying to hang on to the capsized boat as the violent storm works against them. A screaming voice shouts "Stay with it!" as the wind and the rain make it extremely difficult. In a dimly lit scene, the camera shows Buck's hands slipping off the side of the boat as Con yells, "hang on, Buck, stay with me!" Meanwhile, Con runs toward a phone booth and calls Dr. Berger, crying into the receiver, "I need to see you." The frenetic pace of these edited shots subsides when the scene changes to Dr. Berger's office. The camerawork generates fear, terror, and anguish as Conrad relives the nightmare of the boating accident and the death of his brother.

8. How does the camerawork in the final scene of the film make you feel about the future of the Jarrett family?

Conrad awakens to the sound of a cab driving away from the house. He goes downstairs and discovers that his mother has gone back to Houston. He and his dad sit together on the front steps. Cal tries to explain to his son that it's nobody's fault that Beth left. The camera focuses on each face as the two of them intently try to communicate with each other. Conrad tells his father he loves him; they embrace. The camera pulls away to a high angle shot of father and son as the credits roll. The bond between father and son is the last image we see. Beth is literally out of the picture, which may very well indicate the future of the Jarrett family.

TWO SCENES WRITING ACTIVITY

The day after we finished viewing the film, I asked my students to identify two scenes that left a lingering impression in their minds and to explain why in a short written response. From the variety of responses, it is clearly evident that no two people view a film in quite the same way. Different images make different impressions on the viewers. Age, gender, race, and life experience influence our transaction with a text.

MOVIE POSTER PROJECT

As an alternative assessment for this unit, I asked my students to engage in an artistic project. The directions state the following: Now that you have seen and discussed the film, analyzed the cinematography and the performances, and read the review, your assignment is to design an advertisement commemorating the twentieth anniversary of *Ordinary People*. In preparation for the project, I encourage students to look at commercially prepared posters around town. I also have movie ads for current releases posted in another classroom, which I suggest they visit to examine the layouts. The actual project has two components, the visual (advertisement) and the written (copy) portion. In the ad, they must create an image that conveys their experience of the film. They can use people, objects, or abstractions to communicate meaning. I suggest they use magazine cutouts, photographs, computer images (Adobe Photoshop), or original drawings. The copy must include the director, the cast, the studio, excerpted critical reviews (which must be original), and a tag line, which I model from *The Cider House Rules*: "A Story About How Far We Must Travel to Find the Place Where We Belong." A final requirement for the project is a one-page explanation of their creative process. I ask them to consider how they came up with their ideas, how they selected the images, how they went about composing the layout, and whether they were pleased with their execution of the project. This activity incorporates critical thinking skills and requires students to create their own media texts. It also provides a creative alternative to a traditional essay assessment.

Overall, I was very pleased with the results. The most extraordinary ad was made using a digital camera. Andrew replicated the Christmas family photo scene, which we had previously analyzed in class. Acting as director, Andrew planned the shot carefully. He arranged all the props (candlestick holders, a vase of flowers, and a painting) in perfect symmetry on the fireplace mantel to reflect the Jarrett family's sense of order. Next, he told his mother what to wear (blazer and pearls) and what he wanted her body language to communicate. He asked her to clench her fists and to force a smile. He stood beside her in front of the fireplace with his arms crossed, indicating absolutely no connection between them. After all the arrangements were made, Andrew set the timer and took his place on the set. The frozen image clearly reflected Andrew's experience of the film, in which a mother and son are completely estranged.

Nick said, "I enjoyed this project very much because it allowed me to be creative, which was a nice break." Yale responded, "I have never been asked to actually write out my thought process until now . . . as it turns out, my thought process is a lot more involved than I had previously believed." Finally, Regina's comment reinforced my belief that the project was truly worthwhile when she said, "Normally, I don't have a creative process, greatly due to the fact that I am rarely asked to make anything that would require using the right part of my brain." Clearly, these students felt challenged, and they appreciated the opportunity to express themselves creatively.

In this unit on "The Sorrows of Affluence," my students and I visited the Patimkin family in Short Hills, New Jersey, an affluent upper-middle-class suburban community; we spent time with the Weeds, the Hakes, and the Merrills in another affluent community—Shady Hills, Connecticut; and finally, we met the Jarretts, who reside in Lake Forest, Illinois, a picturesque, well-to-do suburban community on Chicago's exclusive North Shore. These stories are about people who live in lavish homes and have memberships in exclusive country clubs, and who live by a certain code of behavior. Maintaining privacy and respectability are necessary rules for survival in places like Short Hills, Shady Hills, and Lake Forest. Divorce, adultery, bankruptcy, alcoholism, and mental illness are unacceptable. Roth, Cheever, and Redford examine such cherished institutions as marriage and the family. Through literature and film, students have the opportunity to go on a journey beyond the closed doors of middle-class America, to investigate the stories of the people who live there.

Additional Writing and Viewing Activities

1. Both *Wall Street* and *Boiler Room* investigate the greed and corruption found in the stock market. Compare and contrast the two films. Consider the complex father/son relationships; the themes of integrity and greed; Gekko's and Young's speeches about greed and money as the root of all evil; and the thrill of playing the odds.

2. No longer are Michael Jordan and Michelle Kwan the only role models for young people. Research a "dot.com" millionaire, a venture capitalist, or an Internet entrepreneur.

3. Research the infamous insider traders of the '80s such as Michael Milken or Ivan Boesky. Watch *Barbarians at the Gate* (1993), which tells the story of a vicious corporate takeover.

4. Screenwriter and director Ben Younger references rap musician Notorious B.I.G. in the opening voice-over from *Boiler Room*. "Either you're slinging crack rock or you got a wicked jump shot. Nobody wants to work for it anymore. There's no honor in taking that after-school job at Mickey D's. Honor is the dollar, kid." Comment on this statement with regard to society today. What are your feelings about the work ethic in the millennium?

5. Interview your grandparents or recent immigrants. Ask them to define the American dream. What values do they feel are important?

6. Watch *Saturday Night Fever* and *Boiler Room*. Compare Tony Manero, who lived for disco dancing in the '70s, to Seth Davis, who lived for driving a Ferrari in the '90s. How do these two films reflect the values of the decades?

7. Read the 1984 Pulitzer Prize–winning play, *Glengarry Glen Ross*, by David Mamet.

    By what system of values do these real estate salesmen operate? Compare Alec Baldwin's role to Ben Affleck's. Compare these salesmen to Willy Loman. What is the moral climate of the play?

8. Compare the different dramatic interpretations of *Death of a Salesman*, starring Lee J. Cobb, Dustin Hoffman, and Brian Dennehy.

9. Compare Tom Ripley, in *The Talented Mr. Ripley* (the story of a poor boy who aspires to live the good life), to James Gatz in *The Great Gatsby*. How has each of these young men reinvented himself? How is Dickie, a scion of a wealthy family, similar to Tom Buchanan? How is Gatsby "great"? How is Ripley "talented"?

10. Theodore Dreiser's novel, *An American Tragedy* (1925), was made into a film titled, *A Place in the Sun*, featuring a Horatio Alger–type protagonist, Clyde Griffiths, played by Montgomery Clift. Compare him to Tom Ripley, played by Matt Damon.

11. Willa Cather's short story, "Paul's Case" (1905), also addresses the theme of the reinvented hero. Paul aspires to wipe out his past and to live the good life using stolen money. Compare Paul to Tom Ripley.

12. The 1950 film, *All About Eve*, is the story of a self-made actress, Eve Harrington, who is not really a poor widow, but rather an ambitious, ruthless, compulsive liar who aspires for stardom. Compare her to Tom Ripley.

13. Compare the film treatment of *Goodbye, Columbus* to the novel. What significant changes have been made? Identify specific cinematic techniques that enhance your viewing.

14. Write a letter to Philip Roth. Address three topics from *Goodbye, Columbus* that are of particular interest to you. Consider his portrayal of middle-class suburban life, modern Judaism, humor, relationships, etc. Use informal English.

15. Read the "Enormous Radio" by John Cheever. Discuss the dangers of eavesdropping into the lives of others. Then, view Hitchcock's *Rear Window* and discuss the companion theme of voyeurism.

16. Critique other film treatments of suburbia: *The Graduate, The Truman Show, The Ice Storm, Pleasantville, Welcome to the Dollhouse,* and *American Beauty*. Relate these films to the theme of the facade of middle-class respectability.

17. In a unit entitled, "Secrets and Lies," students read *A Streetcar Named Desire* by Tennessee Williams and selected short stories by Dorothy Parker. After discussing similarities between the themes of the play and the stories, students were required to view a film outside of class that addressed "secrets and lies." Some titles that worked especially well were: *The Maltese Falcon, All About Eve, Apocalypse Now, The Ice Storm, The Graduate, American Beauty, The Insider,* and *Happiness*.

Videos Cited

High Noon, 1952, Fred Zinnemann, 84 min.

My Darling Clementine, 1946, John Ford, 97 min.

Ordinary People, 1980, Robert Redford, R, 124 min.

Shane, 1953, George Stevens, 118 min.

Stagecoach, 1939, John Ford, 95 min.

Wall Street, 1987, Oliver Stone, R, 124 min.

Works Cited

CHEEVER, JOHN. 1946. *The Stories of John Cheever*. New York: Ballantine Books.

FITZGERALD, F. SCOTT. 1925. *The Great Gatsby*. New York: Charles Scribner's Sons.

MILLER, ARTHUR. 1949. *Death of a Salesman*. New York: Penguin Books.

ROTH, PHILIP. 1959. *Goodbye, Columbus*. New York: Vintage Books.

EIGHT

The Wonder Years *in Literature,*
TV, and Film

ELLEN KRUEGER

If it's September and I'm teaching ninth-grade English, then the curriculum calls for literary genres. The course revolves around themes of coming-of-age and transformation; however, I see no reason to limit our discussions of setting, conflict, theme, plot, point of view, and characterization to those found in short stories and novels alone. Integrating TV and film into an existing curriculum not only complements literary analysis, but also introduces nonprint conventions such as camerawork and editing, and generates lively classroom discussions.

Within the short story unit, we spend several weeks reading and analyzing contemporary short stories by authors such as Amy Tan, Anne Tyler, Kurt Vonnegut, Jr., Aharon Megged, Eugene Collier, and Alice Walker. These stories raise questions about the experiences and people who help shape our lives and guide us on the path toward adulthood. Throughout the unit, students keep reader response journals, which help facilitate our classroom discussions. For example, they often write about the indispensable scene in the story—the one scene without which the story could not exist. By comparing the different scenes they select and their defenses of their choices, a larger issue is raised: What do we, as readers, bring to literature that affects our experience of the text? Race is certainly one significant factor. In Amy Tan's "The Rules of the Game," a young Chinese American chess prodigy feels suffocated by her domineering mother. An Asian reader might empathize more with the plight of the daughter if the feelings are familiar; however, race might not even be an issue at all, considering many young people feel pressured to live up to their parents' expectations. In Anne Tyler's "Teenage Wasteland," the young male protagonist who feels disconnected and misunderstood might appeal more to male readers who feel completely estranged from their families, but this may not necessarily be a gender issue at all. Good literature should engage a reader's feelings regardless of race or gender; nevertheless, these may be issues worth addressing with students. Another factor that contributes to a reader's response is socioeconomic background. Most of my students are white and comfortably middle class, and yet in Eugenia Collier's "Marigolds," we read about a poor, black, southern family. So we explore the universal feelings of fear and uncertainty that young people feel when their home lives lack stability, which may lead them to irrational acts of violence. Keeping a reader response journal encourages students to read beyond plot and to become aware of their roles as readers.

At the conclusion of the short story unit, I also include selections from several TV series, including *The Wonder Years* and *My So-Called Life*, both of which are still shown as reruns on cable stations such as Nick at Nite, MTV, and TVland. Several episodes of *My So-Called Life* are also available for sale at video stores. Reruns on network TV include *Roseanne*, *Fresh Prince of Bel Air*, and *The Cosby Show*. The latest trend in network programming is the obsession with youth culture, as evidenced by choices including *Dawson's Creek*, *Seventh Heaven*, *Popular*, and *Roswell*. After introducing the notion of watching TV in the coming-of-age unit, one of my students, Rachel, said, "If we're taught to analyze what we watch, we'll become more active viewers. We have no problem thinking about TV." In this unit, students were assigned viewer response journals to encourage them to be more consciously involved in their TV viewing. If meaning is negotiated through the transaction between the reader and the text, as reader response theory suggests, then the principle can also be applied to a nonprint text. No two students experience a short story or novel the same way, nor do they view a TV show or film the same way. They must negotiate meaning depending on their personal background, age, gender, or race. Using a viewer response journal (VRJ) helps students negotiate meaning by providing a framework. It also encourages active, rather than passive, viewing because writing is used as an extension of understanding. The media present moments we can share with others.

General Strategies for Critical Viewing

One way to promote visual discrimination and to increase concentration is to select a five- to ten-minute clip from a vintage or current television program. (Always preview the show prior to using it in class.) Ask the following questions:

- What happens in the segment?
- Re-create the sequence of events.
- What did you notice about the camerawork?
- Were there visual/verbal cues used to establish when and where the story takes place?
- How realistic is each character?
- What do you think happens next?

Teachers rarely ask students to comment on TV critically, and yet the criteria for evaluating literature and TV are similar in many ways. For example, in fiction we identify point of view. In "The Rules of the Game" by Amy Tan, Pearl is narrating the story in first person, yet as an adult flashing back on a pivotal experience in her youth. Similarly, we analyze point of view in *The Wonder Years*, a nostalgic look at growing up in the 1960s. The adult voice-over narration of Kevin Arnold comments on the events of the story from a safe distance. The juxtaposition of the adult voice with the youthful voice creates poignancy and humor. One of the questions in the viewer's journal asks students to identify a scene, a portion of dialogue, or a moment that lingers in their minds after the episode is over. When we share responses this time, TV conventions enter our discussion. For example, in discussing the pilot episode of *The Wonder Years*, one student singled out the moment when Kevin and his parents, who had just left the principal's office where Kevin was severely reprimanded for misconduct, arrive home. "And then it happened," says the adult voice-over. Kevin's brother, Wayne, and his sister, Karen, come out the front door to announce that their neighbor, Wayne Cooper, has been killed in Vietnam. Discussing this moment, we investigate how meaning is conveyed visually. The camera zooms in on the shocked and saddened faces of Kevin and his parents. A student pointed to the movement of the camera as it zoomed in on Mr. Arnold's hand pressing down on Kevin's shoulder. What is being communicated visually, we decided, is that in a split second, our entire universe can change. The camera manipulates our emotions by arranging the images and placing the lens in such a way that we feel the powerful loss of a total stranger who could have been one of Mr. Arnold's sons or one of our own relations. Somber music is another convention that emphasizes the loss of Wayne Cooper. The transition from print to TV builds on knowledge students already possess, such as point of view, characterization, setting, and theme, and expands the discussion to recognizable TV conventions including camerawork, lighting, music, editing, pacing, special effects, and even commercial placements. *The Wonder Years* captures the uncharted territory of adolescence. As Kevin's adult voice says, "inside the identical boxes of suburbia . . . families bond together in the pain and struggle of love . . . sharing moments that made us cry and laugh . . . moments of sorrow and wonder." Because students grew up watching these familiar images, they feel a close emotional bond to the characters, which fosters empathy and compassion. Similarly, *My So-Called Life* provides a wonderful opportunity to include another popular TV show into the coming-of-age unit. Whereas *The Wonder Years* was set in white, middle-class suburbia in the late 1960s and featured a typical male junior high school protagonist, *My So-Called Life*, which shares a similar setting, is set in the 1990s and features an ordinary female high school protagonist. According to *New York Times* critic Elizabeth Kolbert's review of the show, Angela "is probably the closest prime time has dared come to the heart of puberty." The technique of voice-over narration is also used, but this time we hear the voice of a young Angela Chase as she negotiates the battlefields of adolescence. She lies on her bed or sits in class and ponders her relationships, her problems, and her life. A viewer-response question I might ask is "What in this episode reminds you of your own life?" Since Angela attends a high school quite like the one my students attend and since their families come from similar socioeconomic backgrounds, this question elicits a variety of responses. For example, one student could identify with Angela's desire to make new friends once she entered high school while at the same time having to deal with her oldest friend, whom she had seemed to outgrow. Another mentioned the need to break away from controlling parents and assert one's independence. Sexuality and relationships with members of the opposite sex were other shared issues. As television critic John Leonard stated, "*My So-Called Life* is intelligent television about people we'd like to know better, the beautiful strangers behind closed doors in a secret room in our own house."

Having already examined TV conventions in *The Wonder Years*, students are aware of the camerawork in this show. For example, one scene takes place during dinner at the Chases'. The camera zooms in on a reaction shot of Angela, whose thoughts are revealed through a voice-over when she says, "I can't bring myself to eat a well-balanced meal in front of my mother . . . it just means too much to her." We all smile because we understand exactly what she is feeling. The close-up shot allows us to read her face, and the viewer establishes an intimate connection with her. The camera then cuts to a medium shot of her parents and Danielle, her younger sister. As we watch this average American family sitting around the dinner table, we once again hear Angela's thoughts in a voice-over. "Lately I can't even look at my mother without wanting to stab her repeatedly." The juxtaposition of what we see and what we hear contributes to the show's realism. Popular, soulful music, such as the ballad "Everybody Hurts" by REM, also contributes to the emotional appeal of this show.

Other shows such as *Roseanne*, which portrays a lower-middle-class, blue-collar family, *7th Heaven*, which portrays a middle-class white-collar suburban family, or *Dawson's Creek*, which portrays a variety of dysfunctional family dynamics, can strongly reinforce the themes we've addressed in literature. As Dayna said, "[Studying] media in the classroom increases our enthusiasm to learn. When we're assigned media work, it's not just anything, it is selected to reinforce what we've been learning." Television provides students with another vehicle to construct meaning, to exercise critical thinking skills, and to evaluate the quality of a production. The co-executive producer of *My So-Called Life*, Winnie Holzman, said in a *New York Times* article (Benenson 1995) that as a writer, she wanted audiences to feel something. "I understand that many people prefer escape on television . . . but there are people of all age groups that are hungry for something that really makes them feel." All of these shows provide quality writing and talented ensemble casts that engage the attention of our students, who are wrestling with the chaos in their own lives.

In addition to using TV in the short story unit, I've also added a film component to the unit on the novel. When I surveyed my students regarding their feelings about studying film, Tommy responded, "the same ideas expressed in literature are expressed in movies, but these ideas go unnoticed by kids. Teaching kids how to view and analyze movies can help them gain insights." Without a doubt, film study belongs in a literature unit. We encourage students to recognize language, style, and meaning in the books we read, and we owe it to them to help them cultivate an appreciation for the visual language used in film as well as the artistic style that filmmakers use to convey meaning. Because film is such an integral part of our popular culture, students should develop the skills necessary to judge its artistic merit as well as its entertainment value. In their own lives, young people are wrestling with identity issues, values, and behaviors. Films dealing with teenagers are powerful vehicles to raise issues and positively contribute to their personal growth.

To Kill a Mockingbird, Lord of the Flies, and *Ordinary People* are three of the novels we read in the coming-of-age unit. Rather than see only films that are based on these classics, I extend the themes of family, prejudice, peer pressure, authority, conformity, and violence to an array of films from which the students and I choose. They know exactly which films best represent them and their struggles. While analyzing the images that Hollywood has packaged, my students explore their own emerging identities. Rachel commented, "It takes intelligence, time, and money to make movies. It's not that difficult to find movies that say something." I asked my classes to brainstorm titles of films that would lend themselves to small-group research projects investigating adolescent themes in coming-of-age films. Among the films chosen were: *Stand by Me, The Breakfast Club, Rebel Without a Cause, This Boy's Life, A Bronx Tale, Lean on Me, What's Eating Gilbert Grape, Welcome to the Dollhouse, Clueless, White Squall, Stand and Deliver,* and *Dangerous Minds.*

Activities That Encourage Active Viewing

Before the small-group projects actually begin, we do a series of activities as a large group, which are designed to encourage active viewing as well as to introduce the conventions of filmmaking. I use the film *The Great Santini* for two reasons. First, it is a film most students have never seen, and second, it reinforces the complex themes of family life in the military (including alcoholism and domestic violence) and coming-of-age, as the young protagonist works through hatred to understanding to love. The lesson examines three pivotal scenes in the film, which convey powerful images of the Meechum family. Before I show each scene, I ask the students to notice how the camerawork affects their experience of that scene.

Shortly after the opening of the film, Colonel Bull Meechum's wife and children are seen standing outside an airplane hangar, anxiously awaiting his homecoming from overseas. Pausing the VCR for a moment, we look at framing (what appears within the rectangular border that frames a shot), arrangement (the placement of the characters and objects within the frame), and placement (the camera's distance from the subject and the angle at which it looks at the subject). The family is shown from a long shot in which they appear as specks. Technical issues such as framing and arrangement are once again reinforced. I ask my students why they think the director shot the scene from such a distance. Actually, the reason isn't clear until we meet the father, who looms larger than life above his family, thus making them all feel inadequate. However, students speculate that the shot will have significance. From a medium shot, Lillian, the mother, instructs the children how to behave when they welcome their father home. She tells them to "get in line—he'll probably hold inspection," and they all walk slowly to meet him. Students notice how the kids stand according to their birth order as if each of them knows his or her place in the family. Once Colonel Meechum appears on the tarmac, they ignore the rules of etiquette and run to hug him. The scene is important because it gives clues to the viewers regarding the complex dynamics of the family.

A second scene takes place on the steps of the family's new home once Bull has been back for a couple of days. A medium shot shows Bull, dressed in full uniform, handling a baton. The camera then pans from left to right showing the forlorn expressions on the faces of his children who once again are arranged in birth order from youngest to oldest. Matt, Karen, Maryanne, and Ben sit on the front steps as Bull announces, "O.K., hogs, this bellyaching will end as of 15:30 hours." He reminds them they are "Marine kids." From a high angle shot, Bull looks down at them and delivers a monologue about how Meechums are "thoroughbreds, winners all the way who excel in sports." The camera then cuts to a low angle shot of Bull's face from the steps as the children look up to hear him say, "A Meechum never gives up." After he "dismisses them," Maryanne says he reminds her of someone from the movies, "but it's not Rhett Butler . . . it's Godzilla." Bull doesn't differentiate between recruits and his own children, whom he refers to as "hogs." Bull's aggressive personality is revealed through the manipulation of the camera. Students can easily make the connection between how the camera is filming the scene and the tension and discomfort they feel as viewers. It is as if we, too, are sitting on those steps being intimidated by a very imposing authoritarian figure.

The third scene is the most disturbing one. It involves a father-and-son, one-on-one basketball game, which ultimately deteriorates into a sadistic competition. I ask the students to notice what effect the camera has on them as we follow the game "courtside." Ben and Bull are framed in a medium shot as they test their strength and endurance against each other, battling for the winning score. Ben says to his father, "Not one of us has ever beaten you in a single game—not checkers, not dominoes, not softball . . ." We feel that this competition is much more than a game. Bull loses to his son, then taunts him by calling him my "favorite daughter" and "my sweet little girl." We feel Ben's pain and humiliation because the camera compresses father and son closely into the frame. Bull bounces the ball against Ben's head as he walks up the stairs, trying desperately to control his rage. Ben finally turns to his father and says, inches from his face, "This little girl just whipped you good, colonel." The camera fades to black as we sigh in relief.

Later that night, in the next scene, Ben is awakened by the sound of a ball bouncing in the driveway. His face is bathed in half light, signifying his confusion. Lillian enters his room, and from a high angle shot, they both look out the rain-streaked window down to the driveway where Bull continues shooting hoops as if he's tying to compensate for his loss. The camera catches Ben's face in half shadow again, as he watches his father. He says, "I was praying we'd all go to war again so King Kong out there could fight someone besides me." The framing and arrangement of mother and son reinforce the strength of their bond. Lillian tries to help her son understand how vulnerable and threatened Bull is feeling because Ben is approaching adulthood. She says, "Don't you think he knows you're up here watching?" For one last moment, the camera zooms in on Ben as he looks down at his father. We, too, are looking through the window down onto the driveway as Bull futilely tries to hold onto his manhood. The scene fades to black.

There is no question that these three particular scenes help to enhance the students' appreciation of the power of the camera on the audience. This shared viewing activity prepares the students to deconstruct the films in the next activity.

Small-Group Presentations

Working in small groups, students were asked to select a film, view it together outside of class, and then prepare an oral presentation based on specific criteria. First, the group had to identify and explain the film genre. Was it comedy, drama, satire, or adventure? We had already defined each genre, so students were prepared to explain, for example, how *Clueless* was a satire of Jane Austen's *Emma*. Next, the group had to provide a general overview of the plot and the roles of the central characters. In addition, they were asked to comment on the quality of the acting as well as the casting choices. Having recently analyzed the filmmaking techniques in *The Great Santini*, the groups were asked to apply this knowledge to their films and to analyze basic camerawork including framing, arrangement, placement, lighting (an effective way to create suspense or emphasize mood), color (another expressive element), sound, and special effects. Finally, each group had to present an overall evaluation of the film in terms of its entertainment value, realism, long-term appeal, innovativeness, and predictability.

Once the presentations began, the classroom transformed electrically. Students became responsible for their own learning. I sat in a seat among the rest of the class while the presenters conducted the lesson. Each group was expected to speak for approximately twenty minutes; however, it turned out that each group required the entire period, if not some additional time the next day. The students analyzed these films with surprising sophistication. They felt an ownership over these movies that target them as an audience and identify their issues—parental interference, family obligations, academic performance, peer acceptance, abusive stepparents, violence, drug abuse, and self-identity. Each group was also required to show clips of special moments in the films that reinforced points they were trying to emphasize. One in particular that I remember was the final scene from *Stand by Me*, in which the two main characters, Gordi and Chris, realize that they have each other to count on when life becomes too complicated. From a high angle shot, the camera shows the boys walking back into town, which looks smaller now than it did before they learned about death, fear, and compassion. As Regina stated, "Since people change after knowledge of the truth, and the boys found out who they could count on to stand by them, they were forever changed." This is a theme we had addressed in terms of Ralph's dynamic change at the end of *Lord of the Flies*, when he discovered the darkness in men's hearts. Making connections between stories, television shows, novels, and films we had shared over the course of the semester became natural for the students by the end of the unit.

On the midterm exam, I posed the question, "In addition to the print texts we've read, which films would you include in our fiction unit?" Justin chose *What's Eating Gilbert Grape?* "This film tells the story of a boy who had to grow up too fast . . . he dealt with family problems like his overweight mother and his retarded brother. Gilbert is faced with a moral dilemma concerning what to do with his brother, Arnie, when his mother dies. The film shows all the qualities of the short stories we've read . . . conflict among family members and a drastic event that brought about a coming-of-age." Kelly chose *Rebel Without a Cause*, and in defense of the film she stated, "I really feel that this film deals with adolescents frustrated with family life, alienated by society, and feeling lonely because there is no one left to talk to." Andy's choice to include in the unit was *Lean on Me*. "Joe Clark comes to Eastside High, throws out all the drug dealers and troublemakers, and becomes a father to many of these children who grew up without a real family, without love, and without security. What Mr. Clark brings is the spirit of hope." Clearly, these students have articulated their passions and insights through these films which, in my mind, justifies a place for film in the ninth-grade curriculum.

Throughout this final unit, I felt great pride listening to these presentations. Because of my own love of film I, too, became an animated participant in our class discussions. This unit added a special dimension to my relationship with my students—one we had never experienced before. Together we explored "the wonder years" of beloved characters in films. Integrating TV and film into a conventional English classroom stimulated critical viewing skills by encouraging students to question, analyze, and evaluate the power and the meaning of moving images. I found my students to be perceptive, sensitive, and observant. I am convinced that their heightened awareness will enhance their ability to analyze literature and better equip them to deal with issues in their own lives.

Additional Strategies for Critical Viewing

1. The premise of the next activity is participating in a shared cultural experience to explore what information we bring to TV viewing that helps us make connections. As a group, brainstorm what students know about the 1950s. Consider social, cultural, and historical events. Then view an episode of *Leave it to Beaver*, *I Love Lucy*, or *The Honeymooners* (all are available on the TVland cable channel or on video). Explore the students' knowledge of the era by discussing this episode. How are men and women represented? How is the American family represented? What do we understand about society at this time, based on the way it is represented on TV? What values are represented?

2. Read selections from *Honey, I'm Home: Selling the American Dream* by Gerald Jones (1992). Discuss sitcoms of the '50s, '60s, '70s, '80s, and '90s as a reflection of social history. An especially interesting show from the 1960s is *The Dick Van Dyke Show*, which portrays the modern American family, the role of the workplace, and the Kennedyesque qualities of the Petries. Students may be surprised to learn that *The Simpsons* is really a parody of the 1950s show *Father Knows Best*. In addition, a discussion of several recent

films satirizing suburbia and the American family such as *The Truman Show* and *Pleasantville* would also contribute to a discussion of how art imitates life. There is no question that television and film reflect the era in which they were produced.

3. Comparing and contrasting literary genres and TV genres fosters an understanding of the similarities and differences between print and nonprint media. First, define genre. Then, brainstorm different literary genres. Next, brainstorm different TV genres. Students can investigate certain types of programming such as soap operas, talk shows, game shows, the news, magazine formats, sitcoms, dramas, police/detective shows, sci-fi, children's shows, etc. What conventions characterize each? What conventions do TV and literature have in common? How are they different?

4. Examine how different professions are represented on TV such as law, medicine, education, religion, media-related, and politics. How accurate are these presentations? Encourage students to interview people they know who actually work in these professions. For example, one of my students' fathers was the chief of police in town. I asked them to sit down together and watch an episode of *N.Y.P.D. Blue* and to record their reactions to the representation of police, minorities, gender issues, violence, and realism. I also invited the chief to come to class and to participate in our discussion. He graciously accepted, and discussed some of the inaccuracies of the production. In another class, one of my students' moms had been an emergency room nurse, and I invited her to sit with her daughter and critique an episode of *ER*. She, too, joined our class discussion and exposed the realities of life in the emergency room as she had experienced them, compared to the way the show represented them. Inviting parents to participate in their children's education is beneficial to everyone involved.

Writing Activities

"It is time that we as a profession not only support the reading of literature, but the making of it." (Donald Murray) This statement can also be applied to the making of nonprint texts. We should support the making of storyboards, TV pilots, parodies, commercials, documentaries, and narrative videos as well. They each provide an alternative form of assessment.

1. One of the most recent and prevalent types of prime-time TV programming is the teen drama in which a group of young people come of age. *Dawson's Creek* is especially popular with young audiences. Encourage students to create their own "pilots" with coming-of-age themes. Viewing television helps students hear dialogue, observe characterization, experience plot developments, recognize conflict, and assess resolutions. Shows such as *Felicity* use

voice-over, which can generate a discussion of point of view. *School Is Out*, an original pilot of a premiere episode written by one of my students, typifies the contemporary dramedy. Unlike the conventional sitcom, the problems of the dramedy are more realistic and are not always solved in thirty minutes. The episode revolves around two brothers—Joe, who has just graduated from college, and Cameron, who is a senior in high school. After the ceremony is over, Cameron is sent to help his brother move his belongings out of the dorm room so they can be loaded in the car. However, when Cameron enters the room, he finds his brother holding the diploma with tears in his eyes. Joe is terrified at the prospects of leaving college, and despite his having graduated magna cum laude with a degree in economics and finance, he has no job prospects. He had put on a big act of smiles and joy just to please his parents. Cameron interrupts Joe and tells him that he, too, had put on an act today. Joe's graduation made him realize that his own was approaching and that he was scared too. The scene ends with the boys leaving the room arm in arm. Both boys felt better knowing that someone else had a problem that was in a way quite different, but in many ways quite the same. The pilot episode of *School Is Out* leaves Joe and Cameron to overcome their fears of life, together, while millions of concerned and interested viewers will tune in every week to find out what happens next.

2. Students can translate a scene from an original idea for a TV show into a storyboard. Each frame would have both video and audio instructions. In a frame from *School Is Out*, for example, the family lines up for a photograph and the camera zooms in on Cameron, who complains that no one made a big deal about his winning the state wrestling championship, but everyone is fawning over Joe's graduation. The scene illustrates Cameron's jealousy of his brother.

3. *The Great Santini* and *Ordinary People* are two extraordinary films that examine families torn apart by emotional or physical abuse. Compare/contrast the father/mother/son relationships in both films.

4. Watch *The Breakfast Club*. Select the teenager with whom you most closely identify and explain why.

5. As a class activity, watch the first scene of *Rebel Without a Cause*. How does a film provide the exposition? Consider the setting, characters, and introduction of the conflict. Compare to the exposition of a short story or a novel.

6. Is Angela Chase, the protagonist of *My So-Called Life*, the Holden Caulfield of the '90s? Defend your point of view.

7. Discuss why there is such an abundance of TV shows targeted for teen audiences.

Works Cited

BENENSON, LAURIE HALPERN. "So-Called Limbo: Now They Really Feel Alienated." *New York Times* 12 March 1995: 40.

JONES, GERALD. 1992. *Honey I'm Home: Selling the American Dream.* New York: Grove Weidenfeld.

KOLBERT, ELIZABETH. "A Female Holden Caulfield for the 1990s." *New York Times* 14 August 1994: 30.

LEONARD, JOHN. "Sensibility and Sexuality, Gossip and Guns." *New York Times* 29 August 1994: 114.

Videos Cited

The Breakfast Club, 1985, John Hughes, R, 97 min.

A Bronx Tale, 1993, Robert de Niro, R, 122 min.

Clueless, 1995, Amy Heckerling, PG13, 97 min.

Dangerous Minds, 1995, John N. Smith, R, 99 min.

The Great Santini, 1980, Lewis John Carlino, PG, 115 min.

Lean on Me, 1989, John G. Avildsen, PG13, 109 min.

Rebel Without a Cause, 1955, Nicholas Ray, 111 min.

Stand and Deliver, 1987, Ray Menendez, PG, 105 min.

Stand by Me, 1986, Rob Reiner, R, 87 min.

This Boy's Life, 1993, Michael Caton Jones, PG13, 115 min.

Welcome to the Dollhouse, 1995, Todd Solondz, R, 87 min.

What's Eating Gilbert Grape, 1993, Lasse Hallstrom, PG13, 118 min.

White Squall, 1996, Ridley Scott, PG13, 127 min.

NINE

Using Film to Enhance Writing

ELLEN KRUEGER

I teach a senior-level elective, Advanced Expository Writing, in which we use the text *Patterns for College Writing* by Laurie G. Kirszner and Stephen R. Mandell. In the introduction, "Reading to Write," they emphasize the importance of reading model essays as a preparation for class discussions, evaluating the ideas of others, forming personal judgments, and developing original points of view. In essence, they say, reading facilitates critical response. They also suggest that the reader actively participates in interpreting the written word based on his or her life experiences, age, ethnic, cultural, and geographical backgrounds. In addition, it is the reader's responsibility to formulate interpretations that can be substantiated by the text. These premises can easily be extended to the use of film to enhance writing on every ability level.

Referring to the *Guidelines for the Preparation of Teachers of English Language Arts,* it is clearly stressed that "students need to construct meaning through different media, analyze their transactions with the media texts, and create their own media texts and performances. Teachers must help students to explore contemporary media as extensions of literature and as entities in and of themselves" (NCTE 1996, 27). The following units demonstrate how I have incorporated these NCTE guidelines into the teaching of expository writing.

Advanced Expository Writing is a course designed to help students improve their writing skills through composing in a variety of rhetorical modes, including description, narration, exemplification, comparison/contrast, definition, and argumentation. *Patterns for College Writing* provides an excellent variety of model essays by such celebrated writers as Sandra Cisneros, Maya Angelou, Joan Didion, Jonathan Kozol, Richard Rodriguez, and Bruno Bettelheim. Their essays are stimulating, provocative, and diverse. However, my students are rarely ignited by what they read, so, as a supplement to these model essays, I use films as texts. This allows students to construct meaning through different media (NCTE Guideline No. 1).

Narration Unit

One of the most accessible modes of writing is narration. To launch the unit, I ask my students to "tell me a story" as a freewriting activity. Topics range from getting a driver's license, visiting a college campus, scoring the winning basket, cutting a class, and attending a rock concert. After sharing these stories out loud, we can discuss several ingredients of narration. Were the events presented in an engaging manner? Did the writer use chronological order, flashback, or begin in medias res (in the middle of a sequence of events)? Were enough details presented to help the audience experience the events? At this point, we turn to our textbooks and read several professional models, including "Finishing School," by Maya Angelou, in which she describes the humiliating experience of working for a white woman; "My Mother Never Worked," by Donna Smith-Yackel, which satirically questions society's definition of "women's work"; and Martin Gansberg's "Thirty-Eight Who Saw Murder Didn't Call the Police," which relates the events leading up to the brutal murder of Kitty Genovese. Reading these essays encouraged my students to listen to other people's stories, to formulate personal reactions to the issues raised, and to develop critical responses to the quality of the writing. However, throughout the class discussions, I could sense that they were not engaged in the writing and were just going through the motions to answer my questions. Turning from the print text to film radically changed the atmosphere of the classroom.

"A quilting bee provides the setting for archetypal tales." This statement accompanied the cast list of the film, *How to Make an American Quilt*, directed by Jocelyn Moorhouse and based on the novel of the same title by Whitney Otto. Since we were sharing people's stories in our class discussions of narrative essays, I selected a film that pieced together the stories of nine women much like the colorful patches in a quilt. The central metaphor worked beautifully for my purposes.

As with any film I show to the class, I carefully screened this one ahead of time. (This must become part of a teacher's preparation for any film presentation.) *How to Make an American Quilt* tells the story of Finn Bennett-Dodd, age twenty-six, who comes to stay with her great-aunt, Glady Joe, and her grandmother, Hy, while she considers her impending marriage and finishes her master's thesis. She spends time with the eight women who meet weekly for a quilting circle and hears their stories.

I prepared some active viewing questions to encourage my students to focus on the stories of these women's lives, beginning with Finn. They were instructed to recreate Finn's story, paying close attention to the details that shaped her life. These details could include bits of speech, descriptions of her environment, and major events in her life. Naturally, being the protagonist, her story continues to evolve as the film continues. One by one, the stories of her great-aunt, Glady Joe, and her grandmother, Hy, as well as the other women in the quilting bee—Sophia, Emma, Constance, Anna, and Marianna—are revealed through flashbacks. Each woman's story unfolds to reveal her in youth and adulthood. The final story comes from Finn's mother, who shows up at the end of the film. At this point in time, the quilt has been completed, and each woman has created a special patch symbolizing her life's story. These include colorful remnants of a party dress, a black crow, two interconnecting circles, the Eiffel Tower, yellow roses, and a painter's palette. Collectively, they reflect archetypal stories. Finn must process what she has learned from these women and their stories and apply it to her own life. In quilting, she is reminded, she must choose her "combinations" carefully, because the right choices will enhance her "quilt." She must remember there are no rules; she must rely on instinct and be brave.

After viewing and discussing the film, I gave my students an assignment to make sure they understood the notion of *archetype* as an original model or type after which other similar things are patterned. I distributed a list of all the women's names, and asked them to explain how each woman's tale was, in fact, an archetype. We shared our responses. I was quite impressed with their ability to understand and apply this term to the film. We concluded that Finn's story was the fear of commitment; Glady Joe was the betrayed wife; Hy lived a life of secrets and lies; Sophia suffered from unfulfilled dreams; Emma was the patient wife with the philandering husband; Constance became the "other" woman; Anna dared to experience forbidden love; Marianna suffered from unrequited love; and Sally learns that with age comes wisdom. Despite their varied and painful stories, the theme illustrated by the patches in the quilt is "where love resides," and is made for Finn's wedding. By the closing scenes of the film, the viewer feels confident that Finn has grown and matured over the summer, and will be able to make the commitment to her fiance that she has been avoiding all along. Throughout our extensive discussions of the film, it became clearly evident that my students were analyzing their transactions with the text (NCTE Guideline No. 2).

Extended Writing Activity: The Interview Project

As Katherine Anne Porter once wrote, "I have never known an uninteresting human being and I have never known two alike. There are broad classifications and deep similarities, but I am interested in the thumbprint." I, too, am interested in the thumbprint. The next step of the process is for students to reflect on their own lives and think about a person they know who has an interesting story to tell. This person would then become the subject of a narrative essay. As we learned through Finn, there are stories all around us.

Among the list of people my students found to interview were a liberated Jew from Mauthausen concentration camp, a victim of a military coup in Brazil, a survivor of the war between India and Pakistan, a woman who was unable to have children, a cousin who abused drugs and alcohol, a substitute teacher who served in the Middle East during WWII, a civilian doctor who served in the Korean War, a minister who attended Martin Luther King, Jr.'s, march on Washington, a grandmother who was a former elementary school teacher, an uncle who worked in the White House during Jimmy Carter's administration, and a mom who organized a protest in her high school in the '60s.

Conducting the interviews was the next step. Reviewing the list of people my students decided to interview, I suggested they formulate several open-ended questions, and begin the interview by asking "What do you remember about . . . ?"

So, for example, if the person survived a concentration camp and emigrated to America, some questions might include "What do you remember about coming to America? being an immigrant? overcoming prejudice, language barriers, and cultural differences?" If the person was a fireman who was badly burned, the student might consider asking, "What do you remember about the events leading up to the call? battling the flames? being injured, and being rescued?" I encouraged them to be sensitive to the feelings of the person they were interviewing, to take notes or record the interview, and not to hesitate to ask for clarification or more details. At the conclusion of the interview, I reminded them to thank the person.

After the information was gathered, the students had to decide how to arrange the events of the story. Reinforcing the strategies we had discussed earlier, I suggested their options were linear, flashback, or in medias res. Referring back to the film, we once again discussed how effective flashback is as a narrative device. This was the strategy most of the students elected to use. For example, in his essay about his mother, who organized a protest in her high school, Ted began his introduction with a general description of the '60s. "Issues like Vietnam, free speech, and civil rights were hot topics of much disagreement, which led to protests, strikes, and walkouts all over the nation . . . students in the '60s had a need to make their voices heard, and often sent their messages using grass root, peaceful means. There were, though, times when that kind of approach simply would not do." His thesis clearly indicates the direction his essay will take. "My mother, Lois, witnessed one of these violent demonstrations in her very own high school, and has lived to tell the tale." The body of the essay sheds light on the circumstances leading up to the demonstration, which include the promise of an assembly to memorialize Martin Luther King, Jr., that which was really intended to be about Archduke Franz Ferdinand II of Austria. "The students' murmurs of disappointment soon grew into roars of outrage." Ted continues to describe the eruption of violence, the evacuation of the building, and the cancellation of school to allow for a cooling-off period. His mother was suspended for several days for "inciting disorderly conduct." He concludes the narrative with a personal reflection about the era and his mother's behavior. "I'd like to think that in some way she helped to accelerate the cultural awareness of Jersey City, even if in a small way, and that her contribution, along with others, led the path to a more enlightened state, which we take for granted today." Through interviewing his mother, Ted had the chance to experience another era, to listen to the rebellious exploits of a parent who was once an adolescent, and to leave the experience feeling inspired. The quality of his narrative essay was exemplary.

Another approach using flashback was the story of Mr. Pannullo, a substitute teacher at our high school, who served in the Middle East during WWII. Eugene, the student writer, was going to cut class the day his science teacher was absent, but changed his mind. "Mr. Pannullo decided that this period would not be wasted on small talk, and decided to teach his own lesson." Using flashback, Eugene re-creates Mr. Pannullo's dramatic story. "A truck with four Arab soldiers pulled up next to their Jeep. The soldiers got out of the truck and drew their guns on private Pannullo and his sergeant." It turns out the Arabs were protecting a field of hashish and thought the

Americans were going to expose them. However, the Americans only stopped to go to the bathroom. Eugene concluded his story returning to the present. "The whole class looked at Mr. Pannullo in amazement, shocked that something like this had happened, and he lived to tell about it." Not cutting class that day was one of the best decisions Eugene has ever made.

A third approach to the assignment involved starting in medias res, which was the choice Andrew made as he re-created the story of his grandfather, Henry, who served as a civilian doctor in the Korean War. Andrew did not want to compose a conventional introduction to tell Henry's story; rather, he began with action.

"Beads of sweat were dripping down Henry's face. A pungent odor emanated from the pack of ten who were trying to stay as invisible as they could. Every few steps up the rocky path of the mountain, the captain, leading the excursion to freedom, would wave his hand wildly. 'Get down, down, down,' he whispered in a strong muffled tone." Andrew composed this dramatic opening to establish Henry's precarious situation in a war zone. Next he flashed back to the circumstances that brought his grandfather to Korea, and then resumed the narrative in a blaze of bullets and explosions. "He could not run; he could not flee. He began to crawl on the ground using his arms and elbows to propel him." Eventually, Henry finds safety.

I was proud of Andrew for challenging himself to find the most creative way to organize his essay. I believe all my students were committed to telling these stories in the most focused, detailed, and emotionally engaging ways possible. Using a film to launch the unit on narrative writing proved to be very successful. It provided a shared viewing experience for all of us, and generated an array of wonderful stories from the ordinary people who populate our lives.

Definition Unit

Building on the success of the narration unit, I decided to use *One Flew Over the Cuckoo's Nest*, directed by Milos Foreman, to expand my unit on the definition essay. Winner of all the major academy awards in 1975, the film, considered an American classic, depicts life in a mental hospital as a frightening microcosm of society, in which power and authority are often abused.

Pre-viewing Activity: Questioning the Hero

It might be helpful to define a few terms as a previewing activity. For example, what is a *microcosm*? Investigate whether the students have experienced this concept before, for example, when they read *Lord of the Flies* or *A Separate Peace*. How is a high school, a college campus, or an army platoon a microcosm? Another important term to define is *hero*. Who are historic heroes? contemporary heroes? mythological or legendary heroes? film and literary heroes? Who are the people we admire for their strength, ability, achievement, nobility, and courage? Have the qualities we once attributed to heroes changed? For example, no one would question that Odysseus was an ancient

119

hero, but do people agree that Hans Solo fits the qualifications today? Do heroes reflect the time and place in which they live, such as Beowulf, or can we modernize the definition to include Chuck Yaeger? A new term for many students is *antihero*, a type of hero who is lacking in traditional qualities such as courage, idealism, and fortitude. The character is frequently a pathetic, comic, or even antisocial figure. He does not possess nobility of life or mind and does not have an attitude marked by high purpose, but often rebels against an oppressive social system. In the character of Randle Patrick McMurphy, students will meet a wisecracking, defiant, rebellious hero, who sacrifices his own life to restore the dignity and manhood of others. Finally, it is important for students to understand the meaning of *mental disorders*, recently defined in a comprehensive new report by United States Surgeon General Dr. David Satcher as "health conditions marked by alterations in thinking, mood, or behavior that cause distress or impair a person's ability to function." Equipped with these definitions, students are ready to begin viewing.

Questions for Viewing One Flew Over the Cuckoo's Nest

Distributing preplanned questions will help guide active student viewing. In addition to following the story line and observing the characters, I want my students to appreciate the film on an aesthetic level. Just as the exposition of a novel or a short story provides essential information, so, too, does the opening scene in the film. When asked to focus on a particular issue, students usually have little trouble responding. The sample responses that follow the guides illustrate how guided viewing questions can help to encourage students to focus on the cinematic qualities of a film.

1. Comment on the information presented visually and aurally in the opening scenes of the film.
   Eerie, Native American music plays as we see a panoramic view of a car driving through the empty wilderness at dawn. The next scene contrasts the calm of the outside world and shows a nurse in a black cape entering a locked hospital ward. The camera pans the sleeping patients. McMurphy arrives at the hospital in handcuffs. The mood is very melancholy.
2. Describe McMurphy upon his arrival at the ward.
   McMurphy is hyper, clownish, bold, and aggressive, and from his exaggerated behavior you can tell he's faking mental illness.
3. What do you notice about the camerawork that helps to establish Nurse Ratched's characterization in the group therapy session?
   Nurse Ratched sits upright and calmly asserts her authority as she begins the session addressing the problems in Mr. Harding's marriage. Her domineering attitude prevails as the men meekly answer her questions. McMurphy sits and observes, but a close-up of his face reveals his amusement at the whole situation. A fight breaks outs between Harding and the others. Another

close-up shot reveals a self-satisfied smile on Nurse Ratched's face as the scene ends.

4. How does the camerawork contribute to the humor during the sequence when McMurphy hijacks the bus to take his fellow inmates on a fishing excursion?

    The camera pans close-up shots of the men from the ward as McMurphy introduces them to the charter boat manager as doctors and professors. Their facial expressions show how they're playing along with him. For the first time in their lives, they feel proud and famous.

5. During the scene after the party on the ward when Nurse Ratched threatens to inform Billy's mother about his sexual behavior, how does the camerawork enhance the dramatic tension?

    Billy is shot close up, and he looks terrified as the nurse speaks to him. He begins to stutter and loses control. Then he is dragged away.

6. Notice the angles used to film the scene when McMurphy strangles Nurse Ratched. Were they good choices?

    From a high angle shot, we see McMurphy strangling Nurse Ratched and we cheer! She's struggling beneath his grip. Billy has just killed himself because of her cruel treatment. She got what she deserved.

Throughout the film, we are exposed to a number of medical and psychiatric conditions. The Chief is a "deaf-and-dumb" Indian. Painfully shy Billy Bibbit stutters incessantly. Dale Harding's intellect prevents him from understanding his wife's adultery. Charlie Cheswick suffers from insecurity and low self-esteem, and a number of other faces who inhabit the ward suffer delusions or have been left in a catatonic state. After each day's viewing, everyone has questions about the psychological problems from which these men suffer. I spoke to my colleague who teaches psychology, and he gave me information about these disorders as well as about lobotomies. It became obvious to me that researching these psychiatric disorders and then writing a definition essay would be one effective way to respond to the film.

Responding to the Film Through Writing

What is ideal about the structure of a definition essay is that it draws on so many other patterns of development. For example, if a student decides to define *lobotomy*, he can also use exemplification to provide examples of people who have had this type of neurosurgery. One student researched Rosemary Kennedy, the sister of John F. Kennedy; Rose Williams, the sister of Tennessee Williams; and Frances Farmer, a Hollywood actress. In defining *obsessive compulsive disorder*, description can be used as a pattern to describe the behaviors of these sufferers. A student found a case study of Greg. "Everyday, Greg feels an urge to wash himself continuously, as if he feels contaminated by germs. His constant washing has already caused the skin on his hands to peel and scrape, yet he continues his washing for long durations of time." Comparison/contrast would be helpful in an essay investigating manic-depression, comparing the extreme highs and suicidal lows of the disorder. From her research, another student describes her aunt's periods of extreme euphoria, during which she mountain-climbed, sky-dived, and bungee-jumped, to the times when she could not lift herself out of bed in the morning and felt utter despair. A discussion of stuttering might involve a process pattern to explain how the flow of speech is broken by repetitions or prolongations of sounds and syllables. Additional topics of interest were anxiety disorders (phobias, panic attacks), schizophrenia (paranoid, catatonic), electric shock therapy, narcolepsy, Tourette's syndrome, and attention deficit disorder. Overall, my students relied on the Internet for researching these disorders. The results were extremely worthwhile.

What about books?

An effective way to respond to the film in a more conventional manner was to encourage students to compose an original thesis and substantiate it using the film. I suggested a number of topics to reinforce issues we had addressed earlier. Is McMurphy a hero or antihero? How is the ward a microcosm of society? How does the film reflect Emerson's statement, "for non-conformity, the world whips you with its displeasure"? What are comic elements in the film? Why is this film considered a modern classic? Why did Nicholson, Fletcher, and Foreman win Academy Awards? Finally, I challenged my students to create their own topics and thesis statements. I modeled one of my own: "McMurphy did more for the self-esteem of the men on the ward than pills, group therapy, or electric shock therapy."

Regina chose to respond to the Emerson quote. In her introduction she stated, "R. P. McMurphy was like a huge boulder thrown into the pool, constantly making ripples. From the day of his admittance to the psychiatric ward, he challenged authority, and for that he paid a high price. *One Flew Over the Cuckoo's Nest* is a parable of how society refuses to tolerate non-conformity." She substantiated her thesis with three concrete examples from the film, including McMurphy's insistence upon changing the daily schedule on the ward in order to watch the World Series, his attempt to break out of the hospital, and his final defiance of throwing a party late one night. Despite his thwarted efforts, "he refused to accept defeat . . . the effort to challenge authority was much more important than the actual outcome. For his behavior, he suffered harsher and harsher repercussions." Regina concluded her discussion, "in the end they worked him until he paid the ultimate price, for they took the only thing Nurse Ratched could never control: his mind." These insights clearly reflect Regina's ability to evaluate the ideas embraced by the film.

Clara wrote about McMurphy as an "unconventional hero who constantly stimulated the patients to be independent during such events as the World Series, a fishing trip, and a party, and ignited a spark of hope into their lives so they could once again feel a passion for life." She also described him as "an outlaw, a hero, and a powerful, unforgettable character."

The single most original approach to the essay was from Andrew, the same student who took a risk in his interview essay, responding to *How to Make an American Quilt* assignment by starting in the middle of the action during which his grandfather struggled to stay alive during the Korean War. Perhaps motivated by the success of that paper, he decided to write an extended metaphor comparing the hospital ward to a military hierarchy, and comparing each character in the film to an assigned order or rank. For example, he identified the military elite as the generals. In the film, he sees the elite in the character of Dr. Spivey, a bureaucrat who is "detached and without a firm grasp of what is truly going on." Next in line after the general is the lieutenant, who has more direct control over his unit of men and who on occasion reports to the general. The lieutenant in the film is Nurse Ratched, who "carries out all ward operations from running group therapy sessions to distributing medication. She must maintain its organization and function." The lowest-ranking people in the military are the enlisted men, who have no individual power and must carry out the orders coming from the officers. In the hospital, the enlisted men are the patients. "They shower when they are told to, eat when they are told to, and sleep when they are told to." Among them, "there are some like Tabor and McMurphy who are drafted . . . and Harding, Cheswick, and Billy who are there voluntarily." Andrew concluded by stating, "The film is a modern masterpiece that portrays the hospital as a microcosm of the military. Everyone was well aware of where they stood in relation to everyone else, but the rebel, McMurphy, blurred those lines. He was impulsive, rash, and aggressive, while the general and lieutenant wanted their enlisted men to be sedate, rational, and passive. His thrilling personality makes him the quintessential antihero. McMurphy's struggle with Nurse Ratched is an archetypal conflict: the rebel versus the establishment, the likable underdog versus the mean-spirited authority, the enlisted man versus the officer. Unfortunately, the system defeats our hero, McMurphy, but his dignity is saved by his friend's courage to end his suffering and commit an act of euthanasia." Andrew's response shows high-level critical thinking, an original point of view, and creativity.

Twenty-five years after its release, *One Flew Over the Cuckoo's Nest* continues to challenge our thinking and inspire our reactions. In an op-ed piece in the *New York Times* (6 January 1999), Maureen Dowd satirizes Elizabeth Dole's candidacy for president: "In politics as in romance, you often crave the complete opposite of your last relationship. Bill Clinton is undisciplined, unruly, untoward. His bawdy appetites and reckless indulgences have been sloshing over our lives for what seems like an eternity . . . what sort of president will we want next? a control freak, of course. Someone who is all discipline and no spontaneity. All trust and no lust . . . After President McMurphy, we will want Nurse Ratched."

Suggestions for Other Films

On occasion, I have also used *The Godfather*, another icon of popular culture, with older students, and received many exceptionally well-written essays. Using this film reinforces one of Kirszner and Mandell's premises, but the application is to the viewer in this case, who actively participates in interpreting a text based on life experiences, age, ethnic, cultural, and geographical backgrounds. For example, Italian American culture is richly portrayed in the film and will generate discussions regarding stereotyping, Catholicism, gender roles, the extended family, respect, and honor. Violence is another pervasive presence in the film, both domestic and outside the family, which fascinates students and stimulates discussion. Finally, cinematic techniques are exceptional in this film. One of my students wrote about Nino Roto's score, which "set a deceptive mood" throughout the film. Both lighting and color are used effectively to create a foreboding mood as the film progresses. Probably the most outstanding film technique used is editing. Juxtaposing certain scenes together, such as in the baptism scene, creates powerful meaning for the audience, and students should be aware of how editing affects their experience of the film. *The Godfather* is considered a modern American classic; however, I would advise exercising discretion and only use it with mature students.

With ninth and tenth graders, I often use *The Breakfast Club*, which is a beloved film among high school students, when I am teaching a unit on characterization. As they watch the film, I ask them to cite specific examples of dialogue, behavior, and interaction with others so they will have material from which to compose character analyses. For example, one student's thesis treats the theme of teenage pressure at home and in school as demonstrated through the characters of Brian "brain" Johnson, John "criminal" Bender, and Andrew "athlete" Clark. After the Saturday detention, the characters feel relief from pressures and reveal secrets that they have hidden for so long. They now know that there are others out there who have the same problems they do. For most teenagers, the messages in this film provide comfort and reassurance. For a personal writing assignment at the end of the unit, I ask my students to select the one cast member with whom they most identify and explain why. This response helps foster a personal connection to the fictional character on the screen, and allows students to construct their own meaning of the film.

Student-Created Media Texts and Performances

In addition to analyzing and evaluating films, I think it is essential that students create their own media texts and performances (NCTE Guideline No. 3).

In my Advance Expository Writing class, I assign two novels—one in each marking period—to be read outside of class. Because we write eight essays over the course of the semester, this project involves an alternative method to responding to literature by creating a live or videotaped performance. Early in the semester, I provide my class with a list of both traditional and modern classics, ranging from *Pride and Prejudice* to *Slaughterhouse Five*, and encourage them to balance their choices between the traditional and the modern. I assign a due date when the reading is to be completed and I distribute a list of "creative responses" to the readings. These are ideas that have worked well over the past few years; however, I am always open to new ideas. Choices include re-creating several scenes from the novel (either live or on video), creating original skits that re-create the novel, creating a talk show or interview, creating dramatic monologues, keeping a journal role-playing through the eyes of a character, comparing the incidents depicted in the novel to the actual events, and pitching a screen adaptation of the novel to a Hollywood producer.

Often students want to work with their friends who have read different novels. I suggest sitting down with them and, together, looking for similarities. For example, three of my students read novels with young adult protagonists: Ben Meechum from *The Great Santini*, Esther Greenwood from *The Bell Jar*, and Johnny Gunther from *Death Be Not Proud*. As each student shared the essence of her book, we concluded that all three protagonists were experiencing severe emotional problems. Ben was the victim of physical and psychological abuse at the hands of his father; Esther was suffering from depression; Johnny was dying from an inoperable brain tumor. We decided that conducting a group therapy session would allow each character to reveal his or her problems as well as to share other aspects of their lives. A friend from outside of class volunteered to help in the role of the therapist, and one of the girl's mom did the videotaping. The result was an extraordinary twelve-minute video. As the class sat watching these three girls role-playing Ben, Esther, and Johnny, we were astounded at how realistically they embraced the fictional characters. They truly stepped inside the skin of these troubled young people without any self-consciousness whatsoever. Because they were improvising, they naturally reacted to each other. For example, after Johnny spoke lovingly of his relationship with his father, Ben revealed his own very troubled relationship with his abusive father. Esther added that she has never really gotten over the death of her father, and had a less-than-satisfying relationship with her mother. Collectively, they presented just the right amount of information to help the rest of the class understand the novels.

Another group that created an extraordinary video read *The Chosen*, *East of Eden*, and *The Great Santini*. They decided to present their troubled protagonists waiting for a train. The exterior shots were filmed at our local train station, while interior shots were filmed in one of the girl's basements. Each girl had prepared a written monologue for her character, which was delivered in a voice-over by another girl while the character paced back and forth on the platform. This decision to use the voice-over was a technical consideration because they wanted to include music and were concerned that if they had spoken, it would have been difficult to hear them. So, accompanying the entrance of each young "man," a song played to establish his character. For example, Hassidic music performed by Itzhak Perlman was heard when Danny entered; a recording of "Cain and Abel" by Louie Armstrong was heard as Cal entered, and when Ben entered, we heard "Georgia on My Mind," performed by Ray Charles. The music provided both an emotional and dramatic touch. After each character was clearly established, all three appeared on the platform. They engaged in the simple conversation of three strangers waiting for a train, while revealing personal information about themselves, their troubled relationships with their fathers, and their uncertainties about the future. As the train arrived off-screen, we heard Louis Armstrong sing a mournful rendition of "Nobody Knows the Troubles I've Seen." Again, I was astounded by my students' ability to understand the psychological complexities of fictional characters so close to them in age, as well as their ability to create such a profoundly moving, original production.

Other clever ideas included pitching *The Time Machine* as a script to a Hollywood producer, conducting an interview with Billy Pilgrim (*Slaughterhouse Five*) with the student playing the roles of both the interviewer and Billy, re-creating the family crisis of discovering the mother has cancer from *One True Thing*, creating an original documentary called *In Search of Holden Caulfield*, in which a filmmaker goes from location to location speaking to people who have known Holden, and interviewing the murderers from *In Cold Blood* and *Compulsion* in an episode of *20/20* titled "Crimes of the Century."

Two other suggestions will enhance this unit. First, I ask the students in the audience to become active listeners. After the presentation is over, they must respond in writing to the question, "How does this presentation make the novels come alive for you?" Then we share their responses with the cast, which is very gratifying to them. Second, I make copies of all the videotapes to use as models in the future. Whether the presentations are videotaped or presented live, this unit provides a welcome break to the writing workshops, and provides students with the opportunity to be creative and to have fun in the process. When asked how they felt about this project, the overwhelming response was favorable. One student said, "I feel that this week has really opened my eyes to a number of books that I would have never even thought of reading if it hadn't been for these presentations." Truly, this activity brings literature to life for the students as well as for me.

Using film in addition to professional essays to teach expository writing reinforces critical thinking skills and helps students to construct meaning through a variety of media. Film promotes lively discussion, and sensitizes students to the cinematic treatment of the traditional narrative. Producing their own videos empowers them to work collaboratively by composing scripts and becoming actively involved in the creation of an original production.

Additional Activities

1. Encourage students to read Whitney Otto's 1991 novel, *How to Make an American Quilt*. In addition to her delightful cast of characters, she provides practical instructions on the art of quilting. Contrast the experiences of reading a novel to viewing a film.

2. Encourage students to read Ken Kesey's 1962 novel, *One Flew Over the Cuckoo's Nest*, and compare the change in point of view from the novel to the film.

3. In addition to *One Flew Over the Cuckoo's Nest*, the following films have portrayed the use of psychosurgery as an instrument of social control: *Suddenly Last Summer* and *Frances*. Research the lives of Rose Williams and Frances Farmer to investigate the people who inspired these stories.

4. Mental illness has always been a popular subject for filmmakers and a source of fascination for filmgoers. Perhaps students will be motivated to see some

of the following: *The Snake Pit, David and Lisa, The Three Faces of Eve, Blue Skies, Shine, Rain Man, As Good as It Gets, Girl Interrupted.* Research the type of mental illness represented in each film.

5. Research Frederick Wiseman's 1967 documentary, *Titicut Follies*, which explores life inside a Massachusetts hospital for mentally ill convicts. The film was censored for twenty-five years because the state of Massachusetts did not appreciate Wiseman's exposure of Bridgewater State Prison's inadequate facilities. Contrast the treatments of mental illness in a documentary to a fictional film.

6. Penny Marshall's 1990 film, *Awakenings*, investigates the strange story of encephalitis lethargica, a "sleeping sickness" that plagued nearly five million people after WWI. Her film is an adaptation of Dr. Oliver Sack's book, *Awakenings*, published in 1973. Research this extraordinary condition.

7. Physical handicaps have also been the subjects of popular films. Two that are exceptional in this category are *The Elephant Man* and *My Left Foot*. Investigating the actual case histories would be a valuable activity.

Videos Cited

The Breakfast Club, 1985, John Hughes, R, 97 min.

The Godfather, 1972, Francis Ford Coppola, R, 175 min.

How to Make an American Quilt, 1995, Jocelyn Moorhouse, PG13, 116 min.

One Flew Over the Cuckoo's Nest, 1975, Milos Foreman, R, 133 min.

Works Cited

DOWD, MAUREEN. "Discipline Us Please." *New York Times* 6 January 1999 A:23.

KIRSZNER, LAURIE G., AND STEPHEN R. MANDELL. 1998. *Patterns for College Writing.* New York: St. Martin's Press.

SMALL, JR., ROBERT C., CHAIR, AND MEMBERS OF THE NCTE STANDING COMMITTEE ON TEACHER PREPARATION AND CERTIFICATION. 1996. *Guidelines for the Preparation of Teachers of English Language Arts.* Urbana, IL: NCTE.

TEN

Developing a Film Elective Course

MARY T. CHRISTEL

Even though this text has advocated the integration of the analysis of nonprint texts across the English and language arts curriculum, it is a natural extension of that integration to create a capstone course that allows students with a special interest in film studies to explore that field of study in greater depth and with greater intensity. Film analysis courses flourished in the late '60s and early '70s in high school programs, but they disappeared by the early '80s as the curricular trend moved away from the proliferation of specialized elective courses to the "back to basics" approach. Any teacher developing this type of elective needs to be mindful of the reasons why such courses disappeared. Administrators feared that these electives were not particularly academically rigorous, and prior to the availability of videotapes, fairly expensive to develop and to maintain. At that time the rental of a semester's worth of 16mm prints of short-subject and feature-length films could mount up to fifteen hundred dollars. Depending on the enrollment in a film elective, that kind of expenditure would not necessarily afford a school system enough "bang for the buck."

Fifteen hundred dollars today would be feasible start-up funding for both equipment and videotapes or DVDs for any course proposal with only a small amount of funding year to year to add to a film collection and maintain that equipment.

Developing an Approach

Like any literature course, a film course needs a framework to organize the series of texts and analytical approaches that will create a sense of academic integrity and rigor and that will convince detractors of its authenticity. As with the study of literature, a historical approach is one of the most fundamental means to build a syllabus, and allows a teacher to examine the breadth of its century long history.

A Historical Approach

The greater availability of silent films in high-quality video and DVD versions affords teachers and their students the opportunity to explore a neglected branch of the industry with films that have inspired classic and contemporary directors. A course following this historical approach could focus on representative films decade by decade and examine how the film industry evolved over time. Selecting representative films in this fashion could prove particularly daunting and, perhaps, arbitrary, so the historical approach might be best served by meshing it with another typical approach, the study of genre. Certain genres reached their peak of popularity and artistry at certain points along the cinematic time line. For instance, the '30s brought with them the Depression, as well as the advent of sound in film. An examination of screwball comedy reflects a popular genre of the Depression era as well as a type of film that depends heavily on dialogue and sound effects to develop its humor. With the '50s came Technicolor; the lavish musicals of this era mesh new advancements in filmmaking technology with a popular taste that reflected a sense of prosperity and well-being.

A Genre Approach

A course that would allow the screening of several films within a single genre could illustrate how that genre developed and has been adapted by contemporary filmmakers. Study could, for example, focus on the classic western in the form of John Ford's *Stagecoach* and compare it to a more contemporary work like Lawrence Kasdan's *Silverado* or Clint Eastwood's Oscar-winning *Unforgiven*. A more unlikely pairing might be a classic western and *Star Wars* to examine how George Lucas' space epic adopts many of the conventions of the classic western genre. Analysis of these film pairings would examine development of plot, characterization, theme, casting choices, and directorial style as these elements appear in the earlier films compared to more contemporary films. Another interesting area to research is the critical reception of these films. A film like *Stagecoach* endeavored to raise the western genre out of the mediocrity of the cheaply made B-movie westerns of the '20s to more narratively and visually sophisticated adult fare. Appendix B at the end of this chapter offers a range of suggested genres and films suitable for high school students.

A Thematic Approach

An approach clearly drawn from literature is the thematic one. A course that explores several themes could offer films from different eras, genres, and directorial styles that illustrate each of the themes. Thematic units could focus on alienation, individualism, the community, rebellion, the personal quest, ethical action, coming of age, the search for justice, or one of countless others. The only drawback to this organizational focus is that it emphasizes a narrative element in film, theme, which could diminish the analysis of the film's cinematic techniques.

An Interdisciplinary Approach

A film course could also draw heavily on how American popular culture responds to the events and concerns that dominate American society in a given decade. This approach could build an interdisciplinary relationship between film and history. The

129

course could begin, say, with the 1920s and a film that reflects or responds to the Depression. Screwball comedies like *My Man Godfrey* or *Bringing Up Baby*, gangster films like *Public Enemy* or *Little Caesar*, and Busby Berkeley musicals including *Footlight Parade* and the many *Broadway Melody* films were all popular escapist entertainments of the time and could provide the springboard to an analysis of popular culture in the midst of economic ruin and personal despair. For the 1940s, the course could focus on the effects of the war in films like *The Best Years of Our Lives*, to examine the painful adjustment for the war hero and his family (especially newly self-sufficient women) at war's end, or it could examine the growing cynicism with urbanization and the corruption of the American dream as treated in detective films like *Murder, My Sweet* and *The Big Sleep*. The 1950s provide the opportunity to examine the allegorical responses to Cold War fears, especially through the cinematic lens of a sci-fi thriller like *Invasion of the Body Snatchers*. The 1960s would then focus on the counterculture movement and the growing disillusionment of America's youth in a film like *The Graduate*. For the remaining decades of the century, students could examine films that rework or reinvent a genre that was popular in a previous decade: the emergence of the gangster film in Francis Ford Coppola's *Godfather* films; the deromanticizing of the soldier in the '80s in a film like *Platoon*; the return of film noir in *Chinatown* in the '70s; the reinvention of the movie musical by Disney in the '90s with films like *Beauty and the Beast*. Depending on the length of the course, teachers could incorporate several films from a given era to compare and contrast the views of American society presented by each genre or film within the same genre.

Resources to Aid in Course Planning

Obviously, no single approach is the clearly preferred method. No single textbook on the market dictates a syllabus of films. Teasley and Wilder's (1997) book *Reel Conversations* offers a useful chapter on the teaching of genres and includes a sustained examination of teaching the western genre that certainly is adaptable to other genres as well. The book also offers a series of chapters on young adult themes that emerge from films, some which could be used as links to other types of films. William Costanzo's (1992) *Reading the Movies* focuses on ten highly teachable films for the high school classroom, which include *Citizen Kane*, *On the Waterfront*, *Rebel Without a Cause*, and *The Birds*. Ralph Amelio's (1971) *Film in the Classroom: Why Use It, How to Use It* may seem dated on the surface but the '70s text focuses on classic films like *Citizen Kane*, *Yojimbo*, and a wide range of westerns as well as a wealth of creative and analytical activities that teachers can easily adapt. Using these books, rather than a textbook, as a guide in choosing films to build a syllabus is greatly recommended, since the texts offer teaching strategies that, especially for novice film instructors, are useful and adaptable. Actually, the lack of a set curriculum in film makes course development particularly exciting and empowering.

A chapter like this is too short to map out all of the films that should be considered by a curriculum team planning a film elective, but it can recommend books that I have found invaluable in developing and adapting the film elective that I have been teaching for the last fifteen years. Two film history books, *A Short History of the Movies* by Gerald Mast and *A History of Narrative Film* by David Cook, are readable informative texts that will provide the novice teacher insights into the development of film from both a narrative and cinematic standpoint. Richly illustrated, both texts provide encyclopedic reference to the major movements, directors, and films that would be included in any high school film course. *Film Art* by David Bordwell and Kristin Thompson is also a very useful resource for teachers because it covers film production, form, style, analyses, and history. For teachers who are considering developing a course organized by genre, Stuart Kaminsky's *American Film Genres* and Thomas Schatz's *Hollywood Genres* provide detailed analysis of key genres such as the western, screwball comedy, the musical, the gangster film, the family melodrama, and the hard-boiled detective film in terms of their conventions, iconography, and tradition within the studio system. The Kaminsky book is especially interesting in comparing Hollywood studio genres, such as the western, to films made in other cultural traditions, such as the samurai film. He also includes a chapter on literary adaptation in *The Treasure of Sierra Madre* as well as a chapter on "Comedy and Social Change." A final book to add to any film teacher's library is *The New York Times Guide to the Best 1,000 Movies Ever Made*. Stuck for a title? Thumb through this guide that includes cast lists, credits, and original reviews from the *New York Times'* noted critics. None of the books suggested here would be suitable as student textbooks, but they are key texts for teacher preparation and reference.

There are also book series that focus on a single film. The British Film Institute has developed as series called *BFI Film Classics*. The series goes through the films chronologically, explaining the key narrative and cinematic techniques used to make each classic a groundbreaking moment in cinema history as well as linking each film to its genre roots and film history. This series is constantly updated with classic and contemporary films such as *Citizen Kane* and *Independence Day*. Rutgers University publishes a series called *Films in Print* that focuses on classic films like *North by Northwest*. This text includes an introduction by the editor/scholar, the shooting script, interviews with the director, reviews, commentary, and a filmography. Cambridge University Press has also started a series of film handbooks that include essays on the aesthetics, cultual context, and cinematic innovations of a single film in additon to a filmography, reviews, and select bibliography. The series presently includes volumes on *Do the Right Thing*, *The Piano*, *Bonnie and Clyde*, and *The Godfather* trilogy. These kinds of text are invaluable to both the novice and the experienced film teacher.

Mainstream Films

In terms of film selection, a nagging issue that all film teachers face is the inclusion of very recent, mainstream films. Students sometimes expect a course of this kind to replicate their multiplex experience and to cater to their tastes. As with any curricular decision, do we want simply to allow students to stay in their cinematic comfort zones or do we want to challenge them with experiences that they may not have without proper guidance and informed selection process? In the introduction to my syllabus I state:

> The overall philosophy of the course is to study films that you would typically not view outside of the classroom in order to broaden your understanding of the development of the art of film and the influence of classic films and directors on modern films and directors.

I design writing assignments that allow students to discuss films that are important to them or that reflect their personal tastes, but I think it is very important not to load a course with obvious crowd pleasers. It is a surefire way to have a curriculum come under fire if it reads like the marquee of the local cineplex from the last few years. In the same way that we expose students to a variety of literary subjects and approaches through a structured curriculum, method and philosophy need to be applied to a film curriculum. There are numerous opportunities for students to look at excerpts from very recent films to illustrate how contemporary directors have adapted techniques from classic films.

Choosing contemporary films raises the issue of whether to include any R-rated material. There really is no all-purpose policy for this concern. Screening certain films in the classroom can be applauded in one community and can result in a teacher's censure or dismissal in another. For example, William Costanzo advocates the use of Spike Lee's *Do the Right Thing* in his book. It might be a thought-provoking and well-crafted film, but in a conservative community its raw language, graphic violence, and brief nudity would not be considered appropriate fare for the classroom. It is wise to examine very carefully the compelling reasons why an R-rated film should be included in a curriculum and to consider what objections could be raised about the content of that film by administrators, students, and parents. Administrators should be particularly aware of potentially controversial material in any course, because no one wants to be blindsided by an irate student or parent. It is wise in most circumstances to obtain parental permission for students to screen a particular R-rated film in class, and teachers should be ready to provide any student who does not receive that parental permission with an alternate assignment. With media's influence on young people's behavior so prominently scrutinized in recent years, there needs to be carefully considered choices of texts and policies governing the use of the texts in place, before a course begins. Teachers should never fall back on the faulty position that students would be watching these films at home anyway, so there would be no problem showing them in the classroom.

As previously stated, developers of film elective courses need to carefully structure a rationale and a framework for the films that are selected. Film classes need to reflect the same balance of genres, time periods, content, and form that well-developed literature classes model. The films chosen need to open students up to film-viewing experiences that they might not necessarily have in the local multiplex or cruising the aisles of the local video store. But once those titles are chosen, what kinds of assignments will lead to meaningful critical-thinking and writing opportunities?

Creating the Necessary Rigor

Film courses should model themselves carefully after traditional English classes in terms of notetaking, reading, writing, and test taking in order to be considered a legitimate course of study. Many colleges and universities balk at accepting film and media courses for English credit, because these classes over time have developed the reputation of only requiring students to "kick back and take in a film" in a fairly passive manner, possibly needing only to give a film a Roger Ebert "thumbs up" or "thumbs down."

Once a teacher or curriculum team decides on the organizational approach for a film, I suggest developing study guides for each film in order to give students an agenda or focus for viewing. That agenda should balance the narrative and cinematic qualities that define a genre, highlight the development of film art, or respond to a specific period or event in American culture. In Appendix C at the end of this chapter, I have included three study guides from early and later points in the course that I teach. The study guide for *My Man Godfrey* focuses primarily on how the film defines the screwball comedy genre and exploits sound to develop its humor. The packet on *Casablanca* focuses on how characters and their relationships are developed narratively and visually. Set time aside not only for the initial viewing of the film but to rescreen selected scenes that highlight critical components of the film's narrative and cinematic characteristics. The study guide for *Bonnie and Clyde* models questions that apply to rescreening key scenes in the discussion of that film. Any feature-length film will need at least five class periods to cover these activities (depending on the length of a given class period).

Teachers should set up a mechanism for students to watch portions of films that they miss due to absences from class. This can be a very difficult procedure depending on the A-V facilities in your school and whether you use videos that are easily available at the local video store. At my school, we do have an A-V department that provides several TV/VCR combination viewers for students to use during their study halls and free periods. I make sure that there is a second copy of a film (in video format) available in the A-V room, and I also require that students fill out a "viewing verification" form signed by one of the adults in the A-V department to make sure that they do indeed watch the portion of the film that is missed. Students can also watch films before school in my classroom. It is imperative that students see a film in its entirety and not just rely on notes or an oral summary from a fellow student.

Assessment

In my culminating activities for a given film or series of films, students include formal essay writing and/or test taking. These assessment instruments need to focus on students' ability to analyze the narrative and cinematic properties of a film. For example, here is an essay topic that I commonly use with my students at the end of viewing and discussing *Citizen Kane*. Robert Carringer, a professor at the University of Illinois and the leading film scholar on *Citizen Kane* and Orson Welles, has developed criteria for judging great films. His criteria focus on three main points.

A truly great film must: *handwritten: — And/or, or, All*

1. make a crucial statement about the culture. It must examine what it is to be an American; what is the American dream; and/or what is an American hero.

2. tell an interesting story in an interesting and appropriate manner (organization, point of view, symbolism).

3. advance the technology of filmmaking by creating new techniques and/or use established techniques in a fresh way (placement, arrangement, editing, optical effects, etc.).

In a multiple-paragraph essay, discuss *Citizen Kane* and apply these elements from Carringer's criteria. Use at least three examples from the film in the body paragraphs.

For an essay such as this, I allow students to use their study guide packets to draw specific examples from the film as part of their support. Books like *Films in the Classroom*, *Reading the Movies*, and *Reel Conversations* will furnish writing topics on specific films, and students can easily adapt those topics to other films as well. I have built essay topics like the one for *Citizen Kane* on notes that I have taken at lectures on specific films and directors as well as from reading reviews or college-level film textbooks.

Writing Topics for Film Journals

Because the class that I teach is named Topics in Composition: Film Analysis, writing must be the focus of class and homework activities, not just the occasional in-class essay test. For the first third of the semester students submit biweekly journals. Initially, I allowed them to write on whatever topics they wished and got plot summary reviews of the latest teen comedies. I have experienced greater success by providing students with a series of topics from which they can choose. I also build in a reading component by asking them to seek out articles on filmmaking and reviews of current films. From time to time I allow them to write on a topic not included on the list. The topics that I have most recently used are included in the following list.

handwritten marginalia: These are really good, but what do you do to develop this criteria? What makes me credible to decide what is acceptable or not?

1. Create a criteria for judging the quality of any film. You need to make sure this method of evaluation goes beyond the narrative (plot, story) qualities of the film. Remember film is a visual (sight) and auditory (sound) medium. As you present your criteria, explain why these elements are absolutely essential to creating a quality film.

2. Apply the criteria you developed in the first journal to either the best or the worst film that you have ever seen. Make sure that you provide for each point in the criteria, by citing specific supporting details from the film. Imagine that your audience hasn't seen the film.

3. Find a review of a film (at least five hundred words in length) that you have recently seen or would like to see. Cut out or photocopy the review and attach it to the journal. Discuss how the review either reflects your opinion of the film or influences your desire to see it. Carefully examine how the critic presents his or her view with supporting details from the film. Include the source of the review and the date that it appeared.

4. Find an article from a newspaper or magazine that discusses a recent or emerging trend in the film industry. For example, *Newsweek* magazine featured an article in its January 20, 1997, issue about the ways *Star Wars* changed the movie industry. Write a summary of and a reaction to the main points of the article.

5. Discuss how class activities have influenced the way you watch films and television. How does the critical attention to the components of film enhance or maybe interfere with your entertainment experience?

When students submit their journals, I only put comments on their work. I want them to focus on their strengths and weaknesses as opposed to checking out the grade. At the end of the journal-writing cycle, I ask students to choose one journal to revise and to evaluate what they have learned about the writing process through this assignment. When students submit their revision and self-analysis, they must also include all their previously written journals. At that time they receive a grade for the entire writing process.

Writing Assignment: Sustained Analysis of a Film

About midway through the semester, I ask students to select a classic or contemporary film that we have not screened or studied in class and to develop a formal, sustained analysis of that film. Students must submit a proposal so that I can approve the films they select to ensure that they are choosing a film with enough sophisticated cinematic elements to sustain such a critical analysis. Some films just don't lend themselves to intense aesthetic scrutiny. Some of the guiding questions I have asked in the past include: Why should this film be included in this film analysis course? What makes it a landmark film in comparison to the films that we have screened in class thus far? How is it significant in its narrative presentation and its use of visual, auditory, and editing effects? The essay then takes on an argumentative position as well as an analytical one. To prepare for writing this essay, students must prepare their own packet for use in notetaking as they watch the film; view the film at least twice; and draft preliminary journals responding to the guiding questions. Then they must write a formal, typed essay, four to six pages in length.

During the final third of the semester, students form small groups and develop a proposal and script or elaborate storyboard for a five- to ten-minute video. This demonstrates their ability to develop a simple narrative and link it with effective camerawork, editing, and sound. I believe it is very important for students to have practical experience in making a short video that helps them apply and synthesize what they have learned during their semester. The school's A-V department is able to furnish the students with the equipment they need, provided that they arrange for the equipment in advance of the deadline. Our supply is not unlimited, but most students do have access to a camcorder or VCR from family or friends. We are able to furnish several editing decks that students can use during their free period and after school. Some students plan their shoots carefully enough that they record their footage in sequence, so their projects require little or no editing. A more detailed description of the project is reproduced at the end of the chapter in Appendix D. We have a class film festival during the last few days of the semester to screen the variety of genres and approaches that result from the assignment.

Final Exam

The school where I teach requires me to use a traditional assessment tool for the final exam in this course. I have developed a multiple-choice portion that requires students to review the film terminology they have studied and mastered over the semester as well as a section that includes several questions about each of the feature-length films we have screened. The questions focus on the contributions made by those films and their directors to the development of film over the last hundred years. Other questions focus on the relationship between and influences on directors from different eras in film history. I also screen *Raiders of the Lost Ark* as the final film for the semester to examine the phenomenon of the blockbuster on the film industry and the way a director like Spielberg draws his inspiration from films of the past. That film then becomes the focus of the final exam essay: Examine how *Raiders* recognizes previous films that set the standard or created expectations for the following elements: characterization of hero, depiction of the battle of the sexes, use of convenient villains, use of documentary techniques, homage to Hitchcock's legacy, adaptations of classic stunts. Select four of these aspects of *Raiders* and show how Spielberg (and company) both borrowed from older films that we have viewed this semester and improved on those techniques. Make sure you carefully balance discussion of narrative and cinematic techniques.

This kind of final exam is really no different in form or content from any other exam that we give in the English department. Nor is the course very different from any other course in the curriculum, except for the in-class screening of visual texts rather than extensive out-of-class reading of literary texts.

It's a Wrap!

Creating a film elective can and will provide any teacher or curriculum team with a capstone course that brings together the viewing, writing, discussion, and critical thinking skills clearly identified by NCTE standards as significant development components of a language arts programs. It also provides meaningful inclusion for students who learn best through visual channels. A film course can be easily adapted and modified from year to year because the cost of purchasing DVDs and videotapes is lower than the cost of adopting a new novel and ordering a copy of the text for every student in the class. Films can be texts worthy of a careful and pleasurable analysis that does not undermine the rigor of the English classroom.

Films Cited

Beauty and the Beast, 1991, Gary Trousdale and Kirk Wise, G, 85 min.

The Best Years of Our Lives, 1946, William Wyler, NR, 163 min.

The Big Sleep, 1946, Howard Hawks, NR, 113 min.

Bonnie and Clyde, 1967, Arthur Penn, R, 111 min.

Bringing Up Baby, 1938, Howard Hawks, NR, 102 min.

The Broadway Melody, 1929, Harry Beaumont, NR, 104 min.

Casablanca, 1943, Michael Curtiz, NR, 104 min.

Chinatown, 1974, Roman Polanski, R, 130 min.

Citizen Kane, 1941, Orson Welles, NR, 120 min.

Footlight Parade, 1933, Lloyd Bacon and Busby Berkeley, NR, 102 min.

The Godfather, 1972, Francis Ford Coppola, R, 175 min.

The Graduate, 1967, Mike Nichols, R, 105 min.

Invasion of the Body Snatchers, 1956, Don Siegel, NR, 80 min.

Little Caesar, 1931, Mervyn LeRoy, NR, 77 min.

Murder, My Sweet, 1944, Edward Dmytryk, NR, 92 min.

My Man Godfrey, 1936, Gregory La Cava, NR, 93 min.

Platoon, 1986, Oliver Stone, R, 120 min.

The Public Enemy, 1931, William A. Wellman, NR, 83 min.

Raiders of the Lost Ark, 1981, Steven Spielberg, PG, 115 min.

Silverado, 1985, Lawrence Kasdan, R, 132 min.

Stagecoach, 1939, John Ford, NR, 95 min.

Star Wars, 1977, George Lucas, G, 121 min.

Unforgiven, 1992, Clint Eastwood, R, 130 min.

Works Cited

AMELIO, RALPH J. 1971. *Film in the Classroom: Why Use It, How to Use It*. Cincinnati, OH: Standard.

BORDWELL, DAVID, AND KRISTIN THOMPSON. 1986. *Film Art: An Introduction*. New York: Knopf.

BUSCOMBE, EDWARD. 1992. *BFI Film Classics: Stagecoach*. London, UK: BFI.

COOK, DAVID A. 1981. *A History of Narrative Film*. New York: Norton.

COSTANZO, WILLIAM V. 1992. *Reading the Movies: Twelve Great Films on Video and How to Teach Them.* Urbana, IL: NCTE.

KAMINSKY, STUART. 1985. *American Film Genres.* Chicago: Nelson-Hall.

KNIGHT, ARTHUR. 1979. *The Liveliest Art.* New York: Mentor.

MAST, GERALD, AND BRUCE F. KAWIN. 2000. *A Short History of Film.* 7th ed. Boston, MA: Allyn and Bacon.

NAREMORE, JAMES. 1993. *Films in Print: North by Northwest.* New Brunswick, NJ: Rutgers University Press.

NICHOLS, PETER M., ED. 1999. *The New York Times Guide to the Best 1,000 Movies Ever Made.* New York: Times Books.

REID, MARK A. 1997. *Spike Lee's "Do the Right Thing."* In *Cambridge Film Handbooks.* Cambridge, UK: Cambridge University Press.

SCHATZ, THOMAS. 1981. *Hollywood Genres.* New York: Random House.

TEASLEY, ALAN, AND ANN WILDER. 1997. *Reel Conversations: Reading Films with Young Adults.* Portsmouth, NH: Boynton/Cook Heinemann.

Appendix A: Sample Film Course Syllabus

Opening Films

excerpts from *North by Northwest* and *The X-Files: The Movie*

Basic Film Terms: A Visual Dictionary

The Art of Film, Vol. 2: "The Camera"

Writing Focus: Apply visual language and basic film terms to sequences screened in class and those chosen by students from films that have had the greatest impact on them.

Early Silent Film Shorts

excerpts from the series *The Movies Begin*, highlighting the work of Edison Studios, Lumiere Bros., Melies, and Porter

Writing Focus: Trace the development of early films from their origins as a novelty to greater visual experimentation and artistry.

Great Early Directors: *Griffith, Murnau, Eisenstein*

excerpt from *Way Down East* (Griffith)

Broken Blossoms (Griffith)

excerpt from *The Last Laugh* (Murnau)

Nosferatu (Murnau)

excerpts from *The Battleship Potemkin* (Eisenstein) and *The Untouchables* (de Palma)

Writing Focus: Analyze the use of more sophisticated editing techniques to expand the narrative and character development potential of visual storytelling.

Genre Study: Comedy

The Art of Film, Vol. 12: "The Emerging Chaplin"

My Man Godfrey (see Appendix C for study guide)

Writing Focus: Apply the characteristics of screwball comedy to *My Man Godfrey* and examine the importance of sound—apart from dialogue—to augment the slapstick humor of film.

Genre Study: Western

Stagecoach

Writing Focus: Analyze how director John Ford relies on the coordination of sound and image to build suspense in the Apache raid and shootout sequences.

Genre Study: Suspense and Hitchcock

The Art of Film, Vol. 7: "Vintage Hitchcock"

Notorious

Psycho

film excerpts from 1998 remake of *Psycho*

Writing Focus A: Apply the characteristics of plot, character, and visual style defined in "Vintage Hitchcock" to *Notorious* and *Psycho* to explore how Hitchcock adapts his own formula.

Writing Focus B: Analyze the party/wine cellar scene from *Notorious* or the shower scene from *Psycho* to examine the visual, sound, and editing techniques that Hitchcock uses to build suspense in these pivotal scenes.

Genre Study: Foreign Film

The Art of Film, Vol. 6: "The Director"

Small Change (French, Truffaut) (see Chapter 6 for study guide)

Cinema Paradiso (Italian, Tornatore)

Writing Focus: Examine how foreign films present narratives that are decidedly working against the conventions and formulas developed in Hollywood films.

Genre Study: Documentary

Nanook of the North (Flaherty)

Nanook Revisited (Massot)

excerpt from *Triumph of the Will* (Riefenstahl)

"The Sixties" (Braverman)

Writing Focus: Analyze the degree to which a documentary presents both objective and subjective material to present its subject matter in a nonfiction format.

Genre Study: Animation

"Remembering Winsor McKay" (John Canemaker)

"Milestones for Mickey" (selected shorts)

"Claymation" (Will Vinton)

shorts featuring Bugs Bunny, Felix the Cat, Betty Boop, and other contemporary works

Writing Focus: Trace the development of animation techniques from the earliest silent cartoons to contemporary computer animation.

American Classics: The Best Films Ever Made?

Casablanca (see Appendix C for study guide)

Citizen Kane

Writing Focus: Develop a set of criteria to describe the characteristics of a classic film and apply those criteria to *Casablanca* and *Citizen Kane.*

Themes in American Films: The Rebel

Bonnie and Clyde (see Appendix C for study guide)

Cool Hand Luke

Writing Focus A: Develop the charactertistics that define the rebel hero using Clyde Barrow and Lucas Jackson as primary examples. Compare the behavior of the rebel hero to heroes in classic films such as *Stagecoach, Notorious, Casablanca,* and *Citizen Kane.*

Writing Focus B: Compare and contrast the use of violence in each film to develop the plot and characterization of the rebel/criminal hero and evaluate the appropriateness of using graphic physical and psychological violence in these films.

The Blockbuster Film

Raiders of the Lost Ark

Writing Focus A: Apply the characteristics of a classic film developed for *Casablanca* and *Citizen Kane* to *Raiders* to determine if a blockbuster film can stand the test of time.

Writing Focus B: Examine how *Raiders* borrows plot development, characterization, visual style, editing techniques, and stunts from films viewed this semester.

Appendix B: Suggestions for Genre Study

Screwball Comedy

It Happened One Night, 1934, Frank Capra.

My Man Godfrey, 1936, Gregory La Cava.

The Awful Truth, 1937, Leo McCarey.

Bringing Up Baby, 1938, Howard Hawks.

His Girl Friday, 1940, Howard Hawks.

The Lady Eve, 1941, Preston Sturges.

What's Up, Doc?, 1972, Peter Bogdanovich.

The Western

Stagecoach, 1939, John Ford.

The Searchers, 1956, John Ford.

Red River, 1948, Howard Hawks.

The Magnificent Seven, 1960, John Sturges.

The Wild Bunch, 1969, Sam Peckinpah.

The Shootist, 1976, Don Siegel.

Silverado, 1985, Lawrence Kasden.

Unforgiven, 1992, Clint Eastwood.

Musicals

Footlight Parade, 1933, Busby Berkeley.

The Gay Divorcee, 1934, Mark Sandrich.

The Wizard of Oz, 1939, Victor Fleming.

Meet Me in St. Louis, 1944, Vincente Minnelli.

An American in Paris, 1951, Vincente Minnelli.

Singin' in the Rain, 1952, Gene Kelly and Stanley Donen.

The Band Wagon, 1953, Vincente Minnelli.

Gentlemen Prefer Blondes, 1953, Howard Hawks.

Grease, 1978, Randal Kleiser.

Film Noir

Double Indemnity, 1944, Billy Wilder.

D.O.A., 1950, Rudolph Maté.

The Maltese Falcon, 1941, John Huston.

Murder, My Sweet, 1945, Edward Dmytryk.

The Killers, 1946, Robert Siodmak.

The Lady from Shanghai, 1948, Orson Welles.

Chinatown, 1974, Roman Polanski.

The Usual Suspects, 1995, Bryan Singer.

Gangster/Crime Melodrama

Little Caesar, 1931, Mervyn LeRoy.

Scarface, 1932, Howard Hawks.

The Public Enemy, 1931, William Wellman.

White Heat, 1949, Raoul Walsh.

Bonnie and Clyde, 1967, Arthur Penn.

Mean Streets, 1973, Martin Scorsese.

The Godfather, 1972, Francis Ford Coppola.

Once Upon a Time in America, 1984, Sergio Leone.

Horror

Nosferatu, 1922, F. W. Murnau.

Dracula, 1931, Tod Browning.

Frankenstein, 1931, James Whale.

Dr. Jekyll and Mr. Hyde, 1932, Rouben Mamoulian.

Island of Lost Souls, 1933, Erle C. Kenton.

The Thing, 1951, Howard Hawks.

Psycho, 1960, Alfred Hitchcock.

The Haunting, 1963, Robert Wise.

The Shining, 1980, Stanley Kubrick.

Halloween, 1978, John Carpenter.

Science Fiction

Invasion of the Body Snatchers, 1956, Don Siegel.

The Day the Earth Stood Still, 1951, Robert Wise.

Forbidden Planet, 1956, Fred M. Wilcox.

2001: A Space Odyssey, 1968, Stanley Kubrick.

Silent Running, 1972, Douglas Trumbull.

The Omega Man, 1971, Boris Sagal.

Planet of the Apes, 1968, Franklin J. Schaffner.

Star Wars, 1977, George Lucas.

E.T. the Extra-Terrestrial, 1982, Steven Spielberg.

Blade Runner, 1982, Ridley Scott.

Appendix C: Study Guides

Genre: Screwball Comedy

MY MAN GODFREY (1936)
Direction: Gregory La Cava

Screenplay: Morrie Ryskind and Eric Hatch

Starring: William Powell and Carole Lombard

CONTENT
Summarize the plot of the film.

FORM
"In the thirties there was a group of films that came to be called 'screwball' comedies, pictures that did anything for a laugh. But while the action in these films was always wildly at odds with any conventional response to a similar situation, most of them had as their point of departure the terrible realities of that period—unemployment, hunger, and fear" (Knight 1979, 265).

- Describe five details from *My Man Godfrey* that reflect the following characteristics of a screwball comedy:
  1. ridicules the rich
  2. reflects the realities of the times
  3. uses verbal wit, rapid-fire delivery, and slapstick (anything for a laugh!)
  4. comments on social conventions
  5. depicts the battle of the sexes

- Explain how the opening scene of the film is particularly effective in introducing the characters and the times.
- The use of sound is often important in comedies, especially in the early sound era. Give three examples of dialogue used to create humor. Give two examples of sound effects used to create humor.
- How does the sound of the following characters' voices reflect their personalities and social position?

  Mrs. Bullock
  Mr. Bullock
  Irene
  Cornelia
  Carlo
  Molly
  Godfrey

- While visual elements are not dominant features of the film in terms of editing and camera movement, subject movement is effective. Comedy that is developed purely through physical movement is called a *sight gag*. Describe two such gags.
- Screwball comedies tend to moralize, sometimes to the point of preaching. How does *My Man Godfrey* fit this characteristic? Cite at least one scene and identify the lesson to be learned.

- Give an example of a modern film that fits Knight's definition of a screwball comedy. Explain how the film fits the definition in a well-developed paragraph. You might want to explore the new "rules" set for the genre in modern films.

Genre: American Classic

CASABLANCA (1943)
Direction: Michael Curtiz

Screenplay: Julius J. Epstein, Philip G. Epstein, Howard Koch

Starring: Humphrey Bogart, Ingrid Bergman, Claude Rains, Dooley Wilson

CONTENT
- Summarize the plot of the film.
- How does the film begin like a documentary? Why use this technique?
- A great film, upon reflection, wastes nothing. Describe the importance of each of the following sequences:

  Ugarte's arrest
  Ferrari's offer to buy Rick's
  Bulgarian refugee couple watching planes leave
  Viktor and Carl at underground meeting

- While making this film, the actors and director did not know what the ending would be or actually how to end the film. How satisfying is the ending? How does it suit the characters and the mood of the film?

VISUAL TECHNIQUES
- Cite three examples of arrangement that clearly reflect the emotional content of the scene.
- Cite two examples where lighting is used effectively to set the mood and/or reflect the emotional content of the scene.
- How are objects used to convey character information or emotions quickly?

SOUND
- How does the use of the song "As Time Goes By" quickly reveal the nature of Rick and Ilsa's relationship the first time Ilsa comes to the cafe?
- Cite two other scenes where the song is used. What do the lyrics reveal about their relationship in the past or the present?
- How is the willingness of some to stand up to the Germans revealed in song?
- How do Sam's songs reflect optimism amid the despair of the refugees? Cite examples of the lyrics of his songs.

- Give two examples of when dialogue provided comic relief. Indicate the speakers in each case.

CHARACTERIZATION

- How is Rick's character treated in the exposition? What do we learn about him? How do we learn this information both verbally and visually?
- How is he visually presented when we first see him? What is he doing? What does this emphasize about his character?
- Cite three examples of details (dialogue, physical business) that clearly reflect Rick's isolation.
- Cite three scenes that illustrate Rick's willingness to commit himself.
- Which relationships that involve Rick depict the following emotions:

  loyalty

  cynicism

  sentimentality

  political ambivalence

- How is the exposition of Viktor Lazlo's character treated? What do we learn about him?
- Compare Ilsa's relationship with Viktor and Rick. What attracts her to each man? Why is she so torn between the two?
- Why is this a no-win situation for all three of them?
- Which two characters primarily provide comic relief? Why is this humor important to the situation?
- In a short journal response trace Rick's transition from isolation to commitment. Use at least five examples from the film that draw on narrative and visual details.

Thematic Focus: Rebel Hero

BONNIE AND CLYDE (1967)

Direction: Arthur Penn

Screenplay: David Newman and Robert Benton

Starring: Warren Beatty, Faye Dunaway, Gene Hackman, Estelle Parsons, Michael J. Pollard

CHARACTER DEVELOPMENT

- List elements of visuals, actor's choices (casting, behavior), action, and dialogue that make the following characters appealing and/or sympathetic:

  Clyde Barrow

  Bonnie Parker

  C. W. Moss

Buck Barrow

Blanche Barrow

- To what extent is the audience meant to feel any sympathy for Texas Ranger Frank Hamer by the end of the film?

DEPICTING CRIMINALS, THEIR CRIMES, ITS AFTERMATH
- How do the opening credits of the film use techniques that try to give the film a documentary look?
- List five ways the film glorifies or glamorizes the exploits of these criminals on the run. Details should be both narrative and cinematic (visual and auditory).
- List five ways the film deglamorizes the exploits of these criminals on the run. Details should be both narrative and cinematic.
- To what extent do you think the film is trying to be a fact-based or myth-based account of the career of Bonnie and Clyde? For example, how does the film change the way Bonnie and Clyde meet and start their crime spree? Why stray from "reality"?
- Nowadays, Bonnie and Clyde would be media sensations (like Mickey and Mallory of Oliver Stone's *Natural Born Killers*). How do Bonnie and Clyde respond to the media coverage of their career? How do they use the media to promote a specific image of themselves as criminals and folk heroes?

SCENES TO RE-VIEW

Bonnie's bedroom

- What visual cues does the scene present to reveal Bonnie's restlessness and feelings of being trapped?
- How is Bonnie presented as being "superior" to Clyde through visuals and dialogue?

Shooting practice at the farmhouse

- What visual and dialogue details reflect the harsh realities of the Depression?
- How does this scene begin setting up Bonnie and Clyde as being the object of admiration to the downtrodden poor of the era?

First bank robbery

- How does the scene effectively use subjective camerawork?
- How does the scene use comic relief? How does this technique influence the viewer's opinion of Clyde?
- What kind of violence punctuates the scene? How threatened or injured are innocent bystanders?

Second bank robbery

- What creates more tension in this robbery in comparison to the first?
- What kind of violence is used in the escape? What is the extent of bloodshed that is left behind?
- What adds a bit of comic tension in the scene?

Third bank robbery

- How is this robbery more "showy" than the other two?
- What does Clyde say and do that will contribute to his status as a hero of the common folk?
- What kind of violence is used in the escape? What is the extent of bloodshed is left behind?
- What kind of comic relief punctuates the robbery and the escape?

First shootout with police

- How does Clyde discover the police's presence? How is it visually presented?
- What makes this scene the most intensely violent of the film by this point?
- How does the use of sound effects intensify the action?
- What are the consequences for the police and the gang of criminals? How much of a bloody aftermath are we shown? Which details are emphasized?
- What might figure as comic relief in this scene?

Second shootout with police and bloody aftermath

- How does this scene begin similarly to the earlier shootout?
- How do the violence and bloodshed escalate in this sequence? What is revealed that makes this scene different in its treatment of violence from the first shootout?
- How does the level of violence seem appropriate or excessive, especially in the second assault the next morning?

Family reunion

- What visual choices give the sequence a dreamlike quality? Why would the director give this scene that kind of quality?
- What background movement serves to foreshadow what will happen to Bonnie and Clyde?
- Which elements in the dialogue foreshadow their death?

Death of Bonnie and Clyde

- To what extent does the murder of these notorious criminals seem excessive?

- Other than the gunshots, how is sound used effectively to build or break suspense of sequence?
- How is time slowed down in this sequence? Is it really slow motion or something else?

Appendix D: Options and Guidelines for a Creative Project

Live-Action Narrative Film

- must tell a coherent story that has a distinct beginning, middle, and end
- employs a cast of actors who can deliver scripted or improvised lines in a focused and effective manner
- use of camera reflects the ability to control focus, movement, and adequate sound recording
- planning and execution of camera setups reflect careful consideration of effective placement and movement of camera as well as arrangement of actors and other elements in a given shot
- editing choices enhance the coherence of the story
- addition of musical soundtrack or sound effects is optional
- bonus: incorporate a visual or verbal leitmotif

Music Video

- select a song that is at least two minutes long and that does not currently have a professionally produced music video in circulation—be prepared to provide a written copy of the lyrics
- select at least five primary sources from film or television from which to draw images
- keep track of the sources of the images—you will need to do a primary source bibliography (for TV footage, you need to know channel, program, and date the program aired; for film title, you need director, studio, and date of release)
- evaluation of the piece will be based on the coordination of the images to the lyrics and tempo of the song

Compilation Film

- requirements same as the music video, but you may choose to add a voice-over narration instead of or in addition to a musical soundtrack
- use a film like *The Sixties* or the Bulls compilation video that we saw in class as a model. As with the Bulls video, you may use more than one song (hopefully just portions of each), so effective transitions between changes in music or voice-over will be crucial

Documentary or "Mockumentary"

- same requirements as live-action narrative film, plus
- for this option you will need to either present a serious approach to a documentary topic of your choosing or spoof the characteristics and purposes of a specific type of documentary

Parody

- same requirements as live-action narrative film, plus
- select famous scenes from movies or TV commercials and re-create them in order to spoof them
- find a framework to link the scenes or commercials together; for example, set up a team of movie reviewers or set up your own commercial break leading out of a spoof of a scene from a TV show that you create

Resources for Teachers

Pedagogy

Burke, Jim. 1999. *The English Teacher's Companion: A Complete Guide to Classroom, Curriculum, and the Profession.* Portsmouth, NH: Boynton/Cook.

> This text covers all the necessary issues concerning the teaching of English including helpful chapters on digital and media literacy that offer concise definitions and practical activities for incorporating these skills in the classroom.

Gardner, Howard. 1983. *Frames of Mind: The Theory of Multiple Intelligences.* New York: Basic Books.

> A seminal work that examines why curricula must address both conventional and less conventional means to acquire knowledge and skill.

Smagorinsky, Peter. 1996. *Standards in Practice: Grades 9–12.* Urbana, IL: NCTE.

> This study applies the standards in language arts to specific texts, skills, and curricular units.

Media Literacy

Alvarado, Manuel, Edward Buscombe, and Richard Collins, eds. 1993. *The Screen Education Reader.* New York: Columbia University Press.

> This collection of essays from *Screen Education* is divided into four sections: film studies, television and media studies, education, and cultural studies. It offers the best ideas from U.K. teachers and theorists with very practical applications to the classroom.

Considine, David M., and Gail E. Haley. 1992. *Visual Messages: Integrating Imagery into Instruction.* Engelwood, CO: Teachers Ideas Press.

> This text outlines what media/visual literacy entails and provides practical suggestions for integrating media literacy activities into a language arts curriculum at the middle or high school level.

DeGaetano, Gloria, and Kathleen Bander. 1996. *Screen Smarts: A Family Guide to Media Literacy.* New York: Houghton Mifflin.

> A primer of concepts and strategies to integrate media literacy into family consumption and responses to the media by focusing on violence, stereotypes, advertising, news, and talk shows.

Fox, Roy, ed. 1994. *Images in Language, Media, and Mind.* Urbana, IL: NCTE.

> The section of the text that focuses on media offers essays titled, "Instant History, Image History," "From War Propaganda to Sound Bites," "Ad Images and the Stunting of Sexuality," "'Don't Hate Me Because I'm Beautiful': A Commercial in Context" as well as a chapter on analyzing visual perception.

Masterman, Len. 1985. *Teaching the Media.* New York: Routledge.

> This text is a comprehensive study of how and why to teach media from a British perspective. It features a comprehensive annotated bibliography of key studies and resources.

Rushkoff, Douglas. 1996. *Media Virus: Hidden Agendas in Popular Culture.* New York: Ballantine.

> The author of The GenX Reader focuses on the intricacies of media manipulation in a brash manner with attention to everything from *The Simpsons* to O. J. Simpson.

———. 1999. *Playing the Future: What We Can Learn from Digital Kids.* New York: Riverhead Books.

> This text examines the impact of children growing up in a media- and technology-saturated environment and emerging with skills that serve them well rather than evolving into callous receptors of media messages.

Worshop, Chris M. 1994. *Screening Images: Ideas for Media Education.* Mississauga, Canada: Wright Communications.

> This is a perfect balance of theory and practice. It provides useful support for developing a curriculum proposal or mission statement for a media literacy program, and it offers useful activities for the classroom.

Representation

Bernard, Jami. 1997. *Chick Flicks: A Movie Lover's Guide to Movies Women Love.* Secaucus, NJ: Citadel Press.

> This text classifies films according to themes that appeal to women, like "female bonding," "perfect love," and "maternal instinct."

Bernstein, Jonathan. 1997. *Pretty in Pink: The Golden Age of Teenage Movies.* New York: St. Martin's Griffin.

From *Fast Times at Ridgemont High* and *Porky's* to *Kids* and *Clueless*, Bernstein examines the explosion of teen films in the '80s and '90s. Chapters treat topics such as "Gross Misconduct," "Dead Teenagers," "True Romance," and "Girls on Film," among others.

Considine, David M. 1985. *The Cinema of Adolescence.* Jefferson, NC: McFarland.

This study acknowledges the relationship between the film industry, the image-making process, and the impact of that image-making on young audiences. Excellent resource for a coming-of-age unit.

Denby, David. 1999. "High School Confidential: Notes on Teen Movies." *The New Yorker.* (May 31).

In a very condensed fashion, Denby examines the current trend in teen films going back to *Carrie* in the '70s and *Heathers* in the '80s.

Douglas, Susan J. 1995. *Where the Girls Are: Growing Up Female with the Mass Media.* New York: Times Books.

An engaging study of the influence of print and nonprint media on women's perceptions of themselves.

Haskell, Molly. 1987. *From Reverence to Rape: The Treatment of Women in the Movies.* 2d ed. Chicago: University of Chicago Press.

This is a seminal study of the presentation and treatment of women in film that is organized chronologically. It also treats the genre of women's film.

Mulvey, Laura. 1989. *Visual and Other Pleasures.* Bloomington, IN: Indiana University Press.

This text presents a sophisticated analysis of the presentation of women in visual images that can be easily adapted to the high school classroom, especially when discussing the objectification of women in film.

O'Barr, William M. 1994. *Culture and the Ad: Exploring Otherness in the World of Advertising.* Boulder, CO: Westview.

A well-illustrated study of how advertising has presented images of race and culture outside of the White mainstream.

Rollins, Peter C., and John E. O'Connor, eds. 1998. *Hollywood's Indian: The Portrayal of the Native American in Film.* Lexington, KY: University Press of Kentucky.

This collection of essays examines the treatment and representation of Native Americans from the earliest westerns to recent films like *Pocahontas* and *Indian in the Cupboard,* two films that influence children's perceptions of Native Americans.

Advertising

Ewan, Stuart. 1988. *All Consuming Images: The Politics of Style in Contemporary Culture*. New York: Basic Books.

> Ewan is the leading expert on the consumer society and on the way the media shape consumer behavior through the construction of powerful images.

Fox, Roy F. 1996. *Harvesting Minds: How TV Commercials Control Kids*. Westport, CT: Praeger.

> A very comprehensive and compelling study of the impact of television commercials on children's attitudes and behaviors.

Ogilvy, David. 1985. *Ogilvy on Advertising*. New York: Vintage Books.

> This illustrated book highlights successful ad campaigns. It explains techniques that work and is written in an anecdotal style.

Twitchell, James B. 1996. *Adcult USA: The Triumph of Advertising in American Culture*. New York: Columbia University Press.

> A study of trends and themes in print advertising that have shaped the consumer culture.

Film

Amelio, Ralph J. 1971. *Film in the Classroom: Why Use It, How to Use It*. Cincinnati, OH: Standard.

> This book is extremely helpful in designing a film analysis class, but it also provides useful ideas for incorporating film into a standard English classroom.

———. 1975. *The Filmic Moment: Teaching Genre Film Through Extracts*. Dayton, OH: Pflaum.

> This book is helpful in exploring how to use excerpts to teach various film genres like the western, horror, science fiction, film noir, the musical, and comedy.

Brode, Douglas. 2000. *Shakespeare in the Movies: From the Silent Era to Shakespeare in Love*. New York: Oxford University Press.

> This volume is the most comprehensive guide to a century of filming Shakespearean plays. Each film is discussed with introductory comments focusing on the nature of the play as dramatic text and its cinematic potential.

Buckland, Warren. 1998. *Teaching Yourself: Film Studies*. Lincolnwood, IL: NTC Publishing Group.

> Originally published in the U.K., this book affords a quick overview of aesthetics, narrative, genres, and documentary films. Buckland also highlights important directors like Welles, Hitchcock, and Scorsese, among others.

Carnes, Mark C., ed. 1995. *Past Imperfect: History According to the Movies*. New York: Henry Holt.

In this volume, historians examine how Hollywood has depicted historical figures and events from Julius Caesar to the Vietnam War.

Costanzo, William V. 1984. *Double Exposure: Composing Through Writing and Film*. Upper Montclair, NJ: Boynton/Cook.

This text offers dozens of approaches for using writing to teach film analysis and using film analysis to teach focused, descriptive, and analytical writing. This is not necessarily a classroom text but an invaluable source book for teachers.

————. 1992. *Reading the Movies: Twelve Great Films on Video and How to Teach Them*. Urbana, IL: NCTE.

This book was released last spring by NCTE and provides valuable approaches to films such as *On the Waterfront, The Grapes of Wrath, Mr. Smith Goes to Washington, Citizen Kane,* and *Awakenings*. The opening section of the book discusses "The Art of Film" as well as "Film in the English Class."

Davies, Anthony, and Stanley Wells, eds. 1994. *Shakespeare and the Moving Image*. New York: Cambridge University Press.

This study offers interpretations of film versions of Shakespearean plays often studied in the classroom as well as an introduction to versions not typically used but easily available on video.

Insdorf, Annette. 1983. *Indelible Shadows: Film and the Holocaust*. New York: Vintage.

This study examines Hollywood and European fiction films as well as documentaries that address the experiences of the Holocaust. Chapters include "The Hollywood Version of the Holocaust," "Black Humor, "The Jew as Child" among others.

Kittredge, William, and Steven Krauzer. 1979. *Stories into Film*. New York: Harper and Row.

This volume includes reprints of the actual stories on which films like *Stagecoach, 2001: A Space Odyssey,* and *The Man Who Shot Liberty Valance* were based. A comparison of a film and its literary form makes for a valuable lesson in a short story unit.

Laybourne, Kit. 1998. *The Animation Book*. New York: Random House.

Here is a nuts-and-bolts guide to how different kinds of animated films are created. It is accessible to both teachers and students interested in how animated techniques have developed since the early days, from pencil-and-paper drawing to high-tech digital imaging.

Mast, Gerald, and Bruce F. Kawin. 2000. *A Short History of Film*. 7th ed. Boston, MA: Allyn and Bacon.

This book should be a staple of any film library. It is comprehensive and very readable.

Penney, Edmund F. 1991. *The Facts on File Dictionary of Film and Broadcast Terms*. New York: Facts on File.

This is a comprehensive dictionary of aesthetic and production terminology.

Teasley, Alan, and Ann Wilder. 1997. *Reel Conversations: Reading Films with Young Adults*. Portsmouth, NH: Boynton/Cook Heinemann.

A practical guide written by two experienced teachers, who present tried and true classroom activities for teachers wanting to use film in the classroom.

Tibbets, John C., and James M. Welsh. 1999. *Novels into Film: The Encyclopedia of Movies Adapted from Books*. New York: Checkmark Books.

A great resource to help teachers research the available adaptations of canonical and popular literature. It offers summary and critique information on each film adaptation.

Television

Barnouw, Erik. 1990. *Tube of Plenty: The Evolution of American Television*. 2d. ed. New York: Oxford University Press.

A comprehensive and readable historical study of the television programming industry.

Bianculli, David. 1992. *Teleliteracy: Taking Television Seriously*. New York: Touchstone Books.

An entertaining look at the impact of television on our culture and attitudes. There are very useful inventories included to "test" your "teleliteracy."

Lee, Martin A., and Norman Soloman. 1991. *Unreliable Sources: A Guide to Detecting Bias in the News Media*. Carol Communications.

A practical guide to identifying the strategies media producers use to shape audiences' responses to stories that also includes contemporary case studies.

Photography

Bustard, Bruce I. 1999. *Picturing the Century*. Seattle, WA: University of Washington Press.

The book collects one hundred years of photography from the National Archives. It provides a rich resource of black-and-white images for their visual composition properties.

Leekley, Sheryle, and John Leekley. 1978. *Moments: The Pulitzer Prize Photographs*. New York: Crown.

This text provides historic context of award-winning photographs, shares the role of the photojournalist, and reveals details leading up to the moment the shutter was hit. This book is scheduled to be updated and reissued in 2000.

Textbooks for Film and Media Courses

Beckert, Christine. 1993. *Getting Started in Mass Media*. Lincolnwood, IL: National Textbook.

> This 120-page text covers all of the major media industries that can be easily used in a high school class.

Bordwell, David, and Kristin Thompson. 1986. *Film Art: An Introduction*. New York: Knopf.

> This is a standard film text for 100-level courses in college. It focuses on film production, form, style, analysis, and history. It is well illustrated and accessible to students who are reading well above grade level. It is an excellent resource for teachers.

Giannetti, Louis, and Scott Eyman. 1991. *Flashback: A Brief History of Film*. Englewood Cliffs, NJ: Prentice-Hall.

> This account of the historical development of cinema focuses on both the American and European film industries as well as briefer segments on Japanese, Australian, and Third World films and directors. It also weaves in examinations of critical genres linked to specific time periods. Readability is approximately grade 15, though suitable for upperclassmen.

Giannetti, Louis. 1998. *Understanding Movies*. Englewood Cliffs, NJ: Prentice-Hall.

> The text focuses on the process of filmmaking with chapters focusing on photography, mise en scene, movement, editing, and sound, as well as chapters on acting and the dramatic elements of film. The final chapter deals with the synthesis of the principles presented through a study of *Citizen Kane*. Readability is approximately grade 14, also suitable for high school upperclassmen.

Johnson, Ron, and Jan Bone. 1986. *Understanding the Film: An Introduction to Film Appreciation*. Lincolnwood, IL: National Textbook.

> This text is one of the few introductions to film that is geared to the high school classroom. The text is planned to acquaint students with various strategies for viewing film in an aesthetic way and evaluating the components of various genres. It also has a brief section on the history of cinema.

Sobchack, Thomas, and Vivian Sobchack. 1987. *An Introduction to Film*. Glenview, IL: Scott Foresman.

> This text is geared to an introductory college course but certainly would be suitable for an elective for upperclassmen. It features sections on the history of cinema, the elements of film, and genre study. The final section of the book features a chapter on writing papers about film.

Writing About Media

Bishop, Ellen, ed. 1999. *Cinema-(To)-Graphy: Film and Writing in Contemporary Composition Courses.* Portsmouth, NH: Heinemann.

> Though geared to teachers of college composition classes, this text offers suggestions of films to use in the classroom, writing activities to support the viewing of those films, and ways to dispel the notion that viewing media contributes to "antiliteracy."

Corrigan, Timothy. 1994. *A Short Guide to Writing About Film.* 2d ed. New York: Harper Collins College.

> This slim and practical volume helps teachers and students to go beyond just examining the literary characteristics of a film to acquiring the terminology and technique to discuss the aspects of visuals, sound, editing, acting, etc. It is effectively illustrated with stills and writing samples.

Roberts, Edgar V. 1995. *Writing About Literature.* Englewood Cliffs, NJ: Prentice-Hall.

> Though the title of this text seems deceptive, it offers a well-developed chapter on writing about film that isn't limited to writing about the literary qualities of film. It also features a sample essay on *Citizen Kane*.

Videography

The Ad and the Ego, 1996, Harold Boihem, California Newsreel, 57 min.

> This fast-paced analysis of the impact of advertising on consumerism will stimulate discussion of how marketing and advertising industries actually conspire to limit consumer choices and undermine our personal values by replacing them with consumer values.

American Cinema, 1994, The Annenberg/CPB Collection, 60 min. per episode.

Volume 1 Hollywood Style/The Star
        2 Romantic Comedy/Film Noir
        3 The Western/The Combat Film
        4 The Studio System/Film in the Television Age
        5 The Film School Generation/The Edge of Hollywood

The first three volumes are especially useful in a film analysis class to acquaint teachers and students with "Hollywood Style" and four significant genres that are accessible for study.

The Art of Film, 1975, Perspective Films/Coronet Films, 20–30 min. per volume.

Volume 1 Screenwriting
        2 The Camera
        3 Performance
        4 Music and Sound
        5 The Edited Image

6 The Director
7 Vintage Hitchcock
8 Performances in Depth: The Many Roles of Alec Guinness
9 The Chase in the Evolution of Movies
10 The Chase as Epic
11 The Role of Women in the Movies
12 The Emerging Chaplin

Volumes 2, 4, 5, 6, and 7 are very useful in their presentation of clips and commentary to inform students about key cinematic techniques and the way a director creates a signature style.

Basic Film Terms: A Visual Dictionary, 1970, Sheldon Renan, Pyramid Films, 14 min.

This is the first film that should begin a collection of video texts that help teachers and students master the key visual, sound, and editing techniques in a very concise form.

Business Ethics: Truth in Advertising, 1997, Films for the Humanities, 28 min.

This program examines how hype and image building distort the ability of advertising to be "truthful" through examples and interviews with advertising executives.

The Celluloid Closet, 1995, Rob Epstein, Telling Pictures/HBO, 102 min.

Starting with silent films, this documentary focuses decade by decade on the representation of gays and lesbians in mainstream films and the efforts of the Hollywood censorship apparatus to contain and control the depiction of homosexual characters and lifestyles.

Color Adjustment, 1991, Marlon Riggs, California Newsreel, 87 min.

As cited in the chapter on representation, this is an insightful study of the depiction of Blacks on TV from *Amos and Andy* to *The Cosby Show*. It can easily be shown in its entirety or shown decade by decade as it applies to a specific unit or course of study.

Consuming Images, 1994, Films for Humanities, 60 min.

This segment of The Public Mind series features Neil Postman and Stuart Ewan in a study of the influence of advertising on the American consciousness and consumer behavior. It clues students in on the deceptive practices of the print and TV advertising industry.

Dream Worlds II, 1996, Sut Jhally, Media Education Foundation, 55 min.

This landmark study of music videos examines the roles women played in the first wave of MTV videos in the 1980s. It would certainly fit well in a unit on representation of women in the media.

Game Over: Gender, Race, and Violence in Video Games, 1999, Media Education Foundation, 35 min.

> This program looks at the history of video games, profiles players, examines images of women and racial groups in games, and culminates with an examination of the impact of violent behavior on the players.

Killing Us Softly II, 1995, Jean Kilbourne, Media Education Foundation, 30 min.

> This is the most recent update of Kilbourne's landmark study focusing on the ways women are depicted in advertising and its damaging effects as well as modeling ways women can respond to these negative images.

The Movies Begin, 1994, David Shepard, Kino Video, 85–105 min. per volume.

> Volume 1 The Great Train Robbery and Other Primary Works
>   2 European Pioneers
>   3 Experimentation and Discovery
>   4 The Magic of Melies
>   5 Comedy, Spectacle, and New Horizons

Here is a treasure trove of the first films ever made. For a film course that is organized chronologically, selections from these tapes are natural places to begin.

New Suits: Profile of an Ad Campaign, 1997, Films for the Humanities, 13 min.

> This program is derived from a Canadian series that focuses on media literacy issues. It follows an advertising campaign as it tries to retool the image of a conservative men's clothier to the satisfaction of a very wary client.

Production Notes: Fast Food for Thought, 1986, Jason Simon, Video Data Bank, 28 min.

> This video provides a series of commercials produced in the 1980s for McDonald's, Pepsi, Mars bars, and Pert shampoo, among other products. It screens the commercials in two formats: real time as it aired on TV and in slow motion with a voice-over narrator reading the production notes that accompanied the development of the spot. These insightful notes reveal the agendas of corporations in establishing both an image and the compelling reasons to buy their products or services.

Race and Local TV News, 1998, ABC News, 21 min.

> This program is derived from a *Nightline* episode and would provide a look at choices made relative to representation in the news industry that would complement the study of such representation in the advertising and entertainment industries.

"Self-Image: The Fantasy, the Reality," 1997, *In the Mix* series, 27 min.

> This is a program that is produced in New York City and features teen correspondents. The segments include how advertising and fashion photography shape teens' self-concept and body image.

Slim Hopes: Advertising and the Obsession with Thinness, 1995, Jean Kilbourne, Media Education Foundation, 30 min.

> Jean Kilbourne is best known for a series of programs, titled *Killing Us Softly*, produced over the past twenty years. Here she continues her study of the representation of women's bodies in print and television advertising.

Tough Guise: Violence, Media, and the Crisis in Masculinity, 1999, Sut Jhally Media, Education Foundation, 75 or 35 min. versions.

> This program is divided into two sections, understanding violent masculinity and violent masculinity in action as depicted in entertainment media and in news stories, including the school shootings in Colorado and Arkansas.

Visions of Light: The Art of Cinematography, 1992, Todd McCarthy, CBS/Fox, 95 min.

> This Academy Award–nominated documentary handsomely explores the art of the cinematographer and how he creates the visual style of a film. This text could certainly be shown in its entirety or in segments that are relevant to the study of a particular genre or director.

Sources for Videos/DVDS

Critic's Choice
P.O. Box 749
Itasca, IL 60143-0749
1-800-367-7765
www.ccvideo.com

Facets Video
1517 W. Fullerton Avenue
Chicago, IL 60614
1-800-331-6197
sales@facets.org
www.facets.org

Films for the Humanities and Sciences
P.O. Box 2053
Princeton, NJ 08543-2053
cutserv@films.com

Insight Media
2162 Broadway
New York, NY 10024-0621
1-800-233-9910
www.insight-media.com

Media Education Foundation
16 Center Street
Northampton, MA 01060
1-800-897-0089
mediaed@mediaed.org
www.media.org

Movies Unlimited
3015 Darnell Road
Philadelphia, PA 19154-3295
1-800-4-movies
www.moviesunlimited.com

PBS Video
1320 Braddock Pl.
Alexandria, VA 22314-1698
1-800-344-1698
www.Shop.PBS.org

Poor Yorick: Shakespeare Multimedia
P. O. Box 21146
Stratford Ontario Canada N5A7V4
(519) 272-1999
www.bardcentral.com

Videofinders
4401 Sunset Blvd.
Los Angeles, CA 90027
1-800-343-4727
www.videofinders.com

The Writing Company/Zenger Video
Division of Social Studies School Service
10200 Jefferson Blvd., Room 9711
P.O. Box 802
Culver City, CA 90232-0802
1-800-944-5432
access@zengermedia.com
www.zengermedia.com

Index